50 INTERVIEWS:
YOUNG ENTREPRENEURS

What it Takes to Make
More Money than Your Parents

by Nick Scheidies and Nick Tart
Cover Design by Jennifer Dervaes
Foreword by Shonika Proctor

Wise Media Group
Denver, CO

50 Interviews: Young Entrepreneurs
What It Takes to Make More Money than Your Parents - Vol. 1
Copyright © 2010 by Nick Scheidies and Nick Tart
youngentrepreneurs.50interviews.com

ISBN: 978-1-935689-00-3
Library of Congress Control Number: 2010931081

Published by
Wise Media Group
444 17th Street, Suite 507
Denver, CO 80202

WISE
MEDIA GROUP

First edition.
Printed in the United States of America.

Wise Media Group
Denver, CO

This book is dedicated to all the young entrepreneurs who are reinvigorating the world with their fresh ideas and unstoppable determination.

...and our parents.

FOREWORD

Every day, young people across the globe are starting radical niche businesses. Access to the internet and technology has leveled the playing field, regardless of your age or where you are located in the world. At the same time, the last half of the century has seen more industries become concentrated in the hands of fewer, larger, often global companies. As employment has migrated to these companies, individual people have started creating their own small businesses in order to become self-sufficient and fill the voids left by these large businesses. Today's youth are contributing to this growing number of entrepreneurs.

Nick Tart knows this situation well. I "met" Nick on the social networking site, Twitter, when he was a student at Colorado State University. I remember receiving my first tweet from him saying he was a fan of my work and that he found my blog about teen entrepreneurs motivational. We chatted through Twitter from time to time and I enjoyed following his progress on JuniorBiz.com – but you never really know where all this social networking will lead or if messages of 140 characters really impact the stream of consciousness.

I realized the impact one year later, when I got the opportunity to meet Nick personally and he asked me to write the foreword for this book. It was a tremendous honor, indeed. Nick was finishing up his last year of school and collecting the stories of inspirational young entrepreneurs, seeking to discover their 'why' and their commonalities. After reading *What it Takes to Make More Money than Your Parents* and recognizing several teen entrepreneurs who I have had the privilege to connect with, it's clear that the book will inspire other young people who are trying to fuel their ambition.

In our chats, Nick and I have realized that we have touched

many of the same lives and walked many of the same paths. Being a part of this book is in alignment with our collective vision. Nick has been a pioneer for the new generation of global change makers, thought leaders, activists, creators, and entrepreneurs. In his world, working with hungry young entrepreneurs from around the globe, *innovation happens.*

Today's dynamic and fearless young people grew up immersed in technology, with the belief they could connect with the world *and* control it with the click of a mouse. And so it is. Facebook is their modern day Rolodex, putting them within one degree of separation from anybody they need to know. Corporations did not scare them with the word 'outsourcing', but instead made them more curious about it. And for them, small is the new big, as the web and digital technology have made it possible for a specialty product or service to be produced at a low cost and distributed to most anywhere in the world.

As more young entrepreneurs learn that there are relatively low barriers to entry in business ownership, they are being more aggressive in their entrepreneurial endeavors. They are becoming savvy business owners through peer-to-peer learning and partnering, by pooling resources, and by leveraging their social capital. They have been able to move real dollars through the economic system and establish non-profits and social ventures with their profits – all while creating real impact in the world economically, socially, and philanthropically. Nick is all of the above, entrepreneurial, creative, outspoken with his ideas, and a thought leader. It is just a matter of time before the impact of his work explodes at a more visible scale.

Nick Tart, his co-author Nick Scheidies, and *What it Takes...* will take you into the minds of some of the brightest young business innovators, across a host of industries, in the U.S. and abroad. Discover what makes them tick and what fuels their ambition. Do you see those same qualities in yourself? Go forth in your journey by building from their success, determination, and enthusiasm as you set out to create your own business empire. It's your world, your time, and your terms. You see it, *now be it!*

Shonika Proctor
Pioneer of Teen Entrepreneur Coaching
June 2nd, 2010

TABLE OF CONTENTS

INTRODUCTION

Children are the future.

Yeah. Right. We've heard that so many times that the expression has lost all meaning.

But there is truth in it. Young people see the world with fresh eyes, looking past outmoded systems and prejudices. They embrace change, they dream up new ideas, and they do it all without batting an eyelash. Incidentally, these happen to be the qualities that set entrepreneurs apart.

They also happen to be qualities that are routinely squashed in the public school system. Thinking small, being obedient, and coloring within the lines are considered virtues in the classroom and for anyone looking to get a job in a cubicle. Kids are missing out when no one tells them how much they could achieve by blazing their own trail.

That's why we're so passionate about *What it Takes to Make More Money than Your Parents*. The 25 amazing young people in this book don't just reveal the secrets to their success: they are living proof of the power that young people possess.

All you need is an idea and an internet connection.

The interviews speak for themselves. If you're holding this book, that means you've already taken the first step to realizing your full potential and making an impact in the world. Don't stop there. We can't wait to meet you at the top.

In the mean time, we'd love your support in the form of your stories, suggestions, connections, or celebratory high-fives.

Thanks – you can grab our attention at Nick@50Interviews.com.

Tiny Literary Giant
Adora Svitak, Author of *Flying Fingers*
Redmond, Washington

BACKGROUND

Adora started writing when she was four years old. She hasn't stopped since. At six, Adora received a laptop computer from her mother, on which she quickly amassed a collection of hundreds of short stories and hundreds of thousands of words – typing at 70 words per minute.

At the age of seven, Adora achieved her dream of becoming a published author with the release of *Flying Fingers: Master the Tools of Learning Through the Joy of Writing*. The book featured several of Adora's short stories, along with her writing tips, typing tips, and advice from her mother. At age 11, Adora published a second book, *Dancing Fingers*, with her older sister, Adrianna.

Today, Adora is 12 and she has transformed her writing success into speaking and teaching success. She has spoken at over 400 schools and presented at the annual TED conference. She's also planning a conference of her own, for kids and by kids, called TEDx Redmond. She has been featured on *Good Morning America* and on *CNN*. Adora also maintains a blog and attends an online public school. She is in the eighth grade.

INTERVIEW

Q: What would you be doing right now if we weren't talking?

A: I would probably be on my computer, sending emails. I have speeches coming up in Toronto, Denver, and Boston, so I might be working on those a little bit.

Q: What drove you above and beyond, to entrepreneurship?

A: My love of reading. From a very young age, my parents would read to my sisters and me. I thought that the authors were doing wonderful things. It didn't really matter which author; I looked up to all of them as my role models. I had a giant collection of role models in my life, from the authors that I read to my parents and friends. I think that helped me understand that I could do great things.

I started writing when I was four years old and I really wanted to publish a book.

> **Adora's Favorite Food:**
> **Crepes**

My parents didn't say, "Wait until you're older." They said, "Go ahead." That really allowed me the freedom to get involved and send off my manuscripts to publishers. It was an interesting way for me to learn about the ins and outs of publishing and selling books.

Q: How do you balance your business with other priorities?

A: It definitely helps that I go to an online public school, called the Washington Virtual Academy. That allows me to travel a lot more freely than I would be able to if I went to a regular school. Occasionally when I travel, it interrupts my studies. But since it's an online school, I am able to catch up. Other than that, there haven't really been negative impacts. I have a lot of support in the form of my family and friends when it comes to my writing. I'm extremely lucky to have this wonderful family.

Q: What challenges have you faced specifically because of your age? How has your age helped you to succeed?

A: People sometimes close doors and make judgments based on your age, how short you are, or the way you speak. That's one of the things that I hope to change. When people look at me, they think, "Oh, a little kid who's just walking along and talking to her mom." There are low expectations. But my parents obviously look at my sister and me as individuals who can do great things. Other people just look at me as a kid.

At the same time, being 12 and having published a book makes people think, "Wow, that's pretty impressive." It's not something that I really capitalize on too much because I'm obviously going to grow up. So I hope to make what I do special, as opposed to it only being special because I'm 12.

My age has also helped me in that I'm able to relate to kids at a level that an adult speaker might not be able to do. As a teacher, I'm able to say, "This is what my generation thinks." Having that voice and being able to speak for my peers is definitely an advantage of being 12.

Q: How have people around you reacted to your success?
A: It has been a positive topic of conversation in my family. But at the same time, they never make a big deal about it. It's not like, "Oh my goodness, you've done so much with your life!" It's more like, "Well, that's wonderful. Let's see what more we can do." There are other members of my family, so it's not all about me.

Speaking at TED was an amazing experience because it's a very prestigious, exclusive conference. You see so many well-known people. It was like: Al Gore is sitting behind you, Steve Wozniak is over here, and Bill Gates is walking by. You feel out of place, like, "How did I end up here?" My grandma is a big fan of Matt Groening, the creator of *The Simpsons*, and I told her, "You know, I got to take a picture with him." That was a memorable response – and one that I remember pretty fondly.

Q: How did you plan and organize your business?
A: A lot of it has been pretty spontaneous. But, I know that some kids need a little more organization. For that, you can

ADORA SVITAK

3

use really simplistic tools like Microsoft Word. Sit down and type out, "I want this to happen. I want that to happen." I hope to see a world where there's a lot of open education available and you can just go online and learn what you need to learn. There are some resources that you'll find, sometimes through Scholastic, about how to write. Having access to the internet is one of the greatest things when it comes to writing.

I write every story differently. Sometimes I'll write a really long, detailed outline, with the family members of every single character in a little diagram. Sometimes I'll just sit down and start writing. I'm still struggling. One of my problems with my stories is that I never seem to be able to end them. I probably would have published seven books by now if I could manage to write endings. I am continually experimenting, trying to find the perfect formula. But there's no way that you can be perfect at anything. We can be good at everything – just maybe not perfect.

Q: What is the single most important reason for your success?

A: I cannot emphasize enough the importance of family encouragement – not just for me, but for everyone. A lot of times disparities in education happen because kids don't have the support of their families. My family has always provided that support, along with the books to read. Small things, like reading books to me when I was little, have really made a lot of difference.

The single most important reason my book was published is that I really, really wanted it to be published. Like any author, I received a lot of rejections for *Flying Fingers*. Some of the large children's publishers said, "We don't work with children." That was a little ironic, considering they were children's publishers. But I didn't stop; I had a very stubborn attitude. When I finally did sign with Action Publishing, it was exhilarating.

Q: What would you tell an up-and-coming entrepreneur?

A: Don't be afraid to pursue your dreams because you're worried about what other people might think. That's the least important thing when it comes to following your dreams. The most important thing is whether or not you want to do it. Is this something that you're interested in pursuing?

A lot of people worry about failing. But your measure of success isn't whether or not you make a lot of money. Your measure of success is whether or not you try. If you pursued something that you felt strongly about, then I call that success. Don't use money as the only yardstick for how well you're doing. You also have to ask, "Does this make me feel fulfilled?"

Consider getting your work published – and it

> ***Adora's Favorite TV Show:***
> **World News with Diane Sawyer**

doesn't necessarily have to be a big, thick book. It could be in a magazine. It could be in your school newspaper. It could be in an eBook. There are lots of different ways of getting published. So, explore all of the opportunities – and when you get an opportunity, go for it. You can take smaller steps along the way. You can read your poem at a local place, a bookstore, or a library. That will build confidence and I think that's quite important.

Q: If you had to battle a giant, what weapon would you use?

A: Do my legs count, as I'm running away? Or is there any way that I could sneak a laxative into the giant's food and incapacitate him for the rest of the day? Actually, I would probably get a rope, lasso the giant, and make him fall down. It might be a little difficult, but it would doable.

People are more scared of public speaking than of death. So, public speaking is like this giant that a lot of people see as so

ADORA SVITAK

huge and frightening. I take it step by step and I try to take it down, to make it less frightening. Then, I say, "I can do this."

Q: What do you want to be when you grow up?

A: I would like to continue my writing, teaching, publishing, speaking, and journalism. I am open to a lot of different things, but I definitely want to make a difference in the world. I'm really passionate about philanthropy and speaking on is- sues of global importance. It's an open road. I hope to go to college in a few years and that's my immediate outlook.

> **Adora's Favorite Website:**
> **CNN.com / TED.com**

My writing has allowed me to meet so many more people than I would if I were just an- other 12-year-old walking down the street. It has also al- lowed me to travel to Europe, Asia, and to over 20 states. I love meeting new people who can teach me new things and I love traveling to new places. [Writing and entrepreneurship] has really enabled me to do that.

Q: As the youngest ever TED speaker, you presented about how adults can learn from kids. Why is that important?

A: Kids have a lot of wisdom that adults don't necessarily real- ize is there. Sometimes adults take it for granted that kids don't know a whole lot about the world. Though not all of us kids watch the news every day, we have a lot of inherent wisdom about what's going on. I correspond with this girl who I know in California and she is able to give me all kinds of insights about people, education, and about kids. I'm a kid as well and it even surprises me. Being able to tap into that knowledge is something that adults could use.

Q: How do you think entrepreneurship can change the world?

A: Obviously, everyone knows about Bill Gates and his founda- tion. But, young people have also been able to do tremen- dous things, like Alex's Lemonade Stand Foundation. Alex Scott was a four-year-old girl who had cancer. She started a lemonade stand that raised thousands of dollars for cancer research. Being able to help a cause is something that anyone can do with their business.

When I was selling my book, *Flying Fingers*, in Vietnam, I was able to raise $30,000 for schools. That was through donations from sponsors, but also through a book auction. You're definitely able to do wonderful things when you put your company behind them.

Anyone can change the world. When we think "change the world," we think of presidents, world leaders, and religious leaders – but it doesn't have to be a bunch of old people. Whatever age you are, you have that ability. You can change the world by inventing something or by sharing your views. There's no committee that says, "This is the type of person who can change the world – and you can't." Realizing that anyone can do it is the first step. The next step is figuring out *how* you're going to do it.

Q: Anything else you would like to add?
A: It's important for kids to know, "I can do this. I am fully qualified." All that you need to become an entrepreneur and change the world is a working brain – and pretty much nothing else.

Website: AdoraSvitak.com
Twitter: @adorasv

ADORA SVITAK

"There are two rules for success:
1) Never tell everything you know."

- Roger H. Lincoln

2

World's Youngest Magazine Publisher
Savannah Britt, Girlpez Fashion Magazine
Voorhees, New Jersey

BACKGROUND

Savannah Britt was a published poet by the age of eight. By nine, she was hired as a paid reviewer of children's books for *The Kitchen Table News* – a New Jersey newspaper with a readership of 70,000. But when that newspaper went under, Savannah was left unemployed at the tender age of 11.

Like any great entrepreneur, Savannah pulled herself up by her bootstraps. She started her own publication – a magazine called *Girlpez* – making her the youngest magazine publisher in the world. The magazine features coverage of events, like concerts and fashion shows, along with interviews from the likes of Shwayze, Kevin Rudolf, and Dawn from Dannity Kane. Now 15, Savannah has guided her magazine as it has transitioned to an online-only format at Girlpez.com. She hopes to use her influence to strengthen girls and their communities.

INTERVIEW

Q: What would you be doing right now if we weren't talking?

A: It depends. It's rare that I have a dull weekend where I don't do anything. I enjoy networking with people. That's how you get further in this business. A lot of times, I'm at concerts. In a few weeks, I have fashion week and I will be there – interviewing people, taking pictures, and just networking.

Q: What drove you above and beyond, to entrepreneurship?

A: I like a challenge. I think what drove me to start my magazine was the fact that I was so young and I was doing something that nobody around me was doing. That pushed me, honestly, to start my magazine. I can be a competitive person.

My mom and dad definitely pushed me as well. My dad has published three books and he's a very determined person. If he says something, he's going to do it. He's also optimistic and he does not procrastinate at all. I think he inspired me.

Q: How do you balance your business with other priorities?
A: It's really hard. I'm in all honors courses, so I have to balance the studies with the magazine. I go to school six hours a day and I have basketball practice afterwards. Then I go straight home and [conduct an] interview if I can. Even some Saturday mornings, I'll do interviews, because it's the only time I can squeeze them in. On top of that, I'm currently working on a music project that I'm trying to get attention for from labels.

Somehow I do it all. I don't know how, but it gets done. I've got a calendar in front of me. It's hard, but I make it work. When I was about 14, in eighth grade, I thought that [Girlpez] was putting a strain on me and that I wouldn't be able to focus on grades. But I was able to bounce back. I have always been a very independent person, but I finally sought help from my parents.

Q: What challenges have you faced specifically because of your age? How has your age helped you to succeed?
A: I'm about to turn 16, which is more of a credible age. But I definitely think that my age has hindered me sometimes. Promoters have said, "Maybe this is not the event for you, because you're only 14."

On the other hand, there are people saying the opposite: "We would love to have a young teen cover this event." My age has been helpful in getting my press releases picked

GIRLPEZ FASHION MAGAZINE

up by different publications. Nobody has ever heard of a 14-year-old publishing a magazine and interviewing celebrities. It's something different.

Q: How have people around you reacted to your success?

A: I would say that eighth grade was my toughest year ever. That was when I started doing star-studded photo shoots and handing out invites. I think that people weren't happy with my success because it wasn't their success. I was able to overcome it because I said to myself, "This is only the beginning. There's a long road ahead of you. Whatever people are saying to you, it doesn't even matter."

> *Savannah's Favorite Food:*
> *Greek Salad with Anchovies*

I've also gotten a lot of positive feedback from people in my life. My godfather, who lives in Washington, DC, is still telling me how proud he is. Amy Astley, the editor-in-chief of *Teen Vogue*, sent me a personal letter. It was the coolest thing ever. Somebody so high up in the industry taking the time out to send me a letter was amazing.

Q: How did you plan and organize your business?

A: Basically, I wrote an outline. It was pretty brief, but it covered everything about the magazine: who I want to serve, who it will circulate to, and where I see myself in ten years.

When I was working for the newspaper, it was all about deadlines, deadlines, deadlines. If you didn't hand your assignment in by a specific date, then it wouldn't be published. So, I learned a lot about what deadlines mean to be successful in this business.

Q: What is the single most important reason for your success?

A: God. This industry is dog-eat-dog. There are so many people who are just doing things for themselves. They're not worried about helping you. Without God in my life, I don't even

SAVANNAH BRITT

know where I would be right now. You have to have that faith, spiritually and morally. I'm also thankful for my strong family background.

Q: What would you tell an up-and-coming entrepreneur?

A: Never give up. There were so many points at the beginning of the process where things were going slow. I didn't feel like I was getting invited to the VIP events like larger magazines were. I just wanted to give up. Really, it took almost two years and I'm still trying to give myself a name in the industry. So, it might seem like your hard work is not going to pay off, but it will. Do not give up.

> *Savannah's Favorite Band:*
> *Coldplay*

A common mistake is that teen entrepreneurs don't take advantage of press releases or Google Alerts. The more you put your name out there, the better. Just to get it picked up by one or two people is great.

Q: If you had to battle a giant, what weapon would you use?

A: Maybe a sword. I think that fencing is cool, so, I would like to fence with the giant. The swords criss-crossing, you're swatting at the giant. As it relates to my business, people in the industry are swatting at me to get where they need to be. The sword is like me weaving my way through, to get to the end, and knocking off anybody who gets in my way.

Q: What do you want to be when you grow up?

A: I want to be a Hollywood publicist and open up my own firm in New York or L.A. where I will work with celebrity clients and plan VIP events.

When I am interviewing celebrities, I have to go through their publicists to arrange the interviews. So, I'm building these strong relationships with publicists at all these firms. It's really cool because I know that after I graduate from college, I will have all of these people who I can turn to and say, "Hey, remember me?" Then, they can help me with my public relations career.

Q: **You've met some big-time celebrities including Sean Kingston, Lil Wayne, and Leona Lewis. How have these celebrities reacted to your success?**

A: They think it is kind of cool. A lot of them say, "You're how old?" They just can't believe it.

Q: **What would you say to a girl who is hesitant to get into entrepreneurship?**

A: There is no reason to be hesitant. I know they might be nervous, they might be shy, and they might want to give up after their first try – but becoming an entrepreneur is a learning experience. You are going to use a lot of the things that you learn now as an entrepreneur when you're an adult. Just try it. If you don't like it, then you can stop – but at least you will be able to say that you tried. And it's fun.

Q: **Anything else you would like to add?**

A: I would like to raise money for Haiti [following the earthquake in January, 2010]. It's a sad experience that's going on there, but it's definitely something that I want to address. It's a wake-up call for the world that there a lot of people who are stricken by poverty.

On top of that, I'm working with another young entrepreneur who runs a blog, Jayswag.com. We want to put together a conference that will feature people in the industry who are well-versed in hip-hop. We want to have a panel of them and let teens ask questions and have a discussion. There are some things in the hip-hop industry that go under the rug and they need to be addressed – like the way they portray women in the music videos, the people they put in the ads, and whether or not their skin color matters. It's something that needs to be discussed.

SAVANNAH BRITT

Website: www.girlpez.com
Twitter: @savlovesyou

> *"Savannah Britt is a good friend of mine. At first glance, you see how Savannah works hard to achieve what she wants. But when you get to know her, you realize that she really cares about what is going on. Congratulations to her and I know we will be hearing more from her, not only in the short-term, but in the long-run as well!"*
>
> ~ **John P,**
> **Comment on JuniorBiz**

2008 Young Inventor of the Year
Philip Hartman, Steam Viper
Loveland, Colorado

BACKGROUND
Philip Hartman became an entrepreneur when he was eight years old. That's when he started building slingshots that shot both BBs and arrows. Today, a home-schooled high school senior at the ripe age of 15, Philip spends most of his time cultivating two somewhat more advanced entrepreneurial ventures.

The first is a new system for fusing optical fibers that is cheaper, more efficient, and more dependable – an invention for which Philip won the 2008 *Young Inventor of the Year* award. The other is called Steam Viper. It's a device that emits steam onto a windshield and is capable of defrosting a frost-covered windshield in about 15 seconds.

INTERVIEW
Q: What would you be doing right now if we weren't talking?
A: I would probably be following up on emails, making phone calls, or meeting with potential investors and marketers for Steam Viper. There are a lot of people involved in making a project happen.

Q: What drove you above and beyond, to entrepreneurship?
A: Most teenagers today think of their only responsibility as getting schoolwork done and everything else is for pleasure. But there's no reason why I can't get a full business running now just because I'm young. I'm willing to spend my school years developing a business.

My dad has really encouraged me to be entrepreneurial ever since I was little. He always showed me articles about young entrepreneurs, along with other things to try to encourage me towards that path.

Q: How do you balance your business with other priorities?
A: I would say that family comes first. Our family is a pretty laid-back family. We're not as busy as a lot of people, which allows me a lot of time to work on my business.

As far as school goes, I don't spend as much time now because I'm a senior. I'm mainly taking AP courses and I probably spend no more than an hour or two a day for school. I wake up in the morning knowing what I need to learn and then I just do my homework. Nobody needs to set me out a plan for my day.

With work, some weeks there isn't much going on because I'm waiting for one thing or another. And then another week I'll be swamped. I usually spend at least five or six hours a day working on the Steam Viper.

Q: What challenges have you faced specifically because of your age? How has your age helped you to succeed?
A: A lot of people don't take you seriously. They don't really trust a youth as much. One of the biggest challenges is working with the government, corporations, and getting business/banking accounts all set up. Until you're 18, if you sign a contract and you want to completely void that contract, you can. Because of that law, it's tricky to get quality investors together. It has been challenging to work around the laws so that I can maintain full ownership of the company, when I can't technically own anything.

But there are a lot of opportunities for young people that don't exist once you turn 21. My age has helped a lot in get-

STEAM VIPER

ting media and attention. There are also many contests for youth that award large grants.

Q: How have people around you reacted to your success?

A: For my immediate family, this is just normal life. So there's no special response. I have a lot of different sections of my life. I play tennis and I also play banjo. In those groups, people don't know that I'm an inventor and entrepreneur. So it's kind of funny when they see me on the news or in a magazine. It surprises most of them because they think that I'm just involved in whatever they're involved in.

For most people, the Steam Viper is really exciting. Everybody knows what it's like to be driving down the road and have bugs all over your window. 20% of all accidents are caused by glare from stuff on the windshield. We also know what it's like to scrape our windshield in the morning. The Steam Viper completely eliminates all of that.

> **Philip's Favorite Band:**
> **Alison Krauss & Union Station**

Q: How did you plan and organize your business?

A: I've never taken a business course, but I've always had an intuition for business. I've made business plans and I've had some different consultants, including my dad, but the way I learn how to do something is just to go ahead and do it. It's the best tool there is. I learn more every time. I could never learn what I'm learning at college. They don't teach it there, because it can't be learned in that way.

Q: What is the single most important reason for your success?

A: Having supportive parents and family has been huge. I definitely could not have done what I did with fiber optics without my dad. Being young is a huge advantage because I've got a place to live, food to eat, and all I have to worry about financially is funding my business. Then, I think it really just comes down to my attitude: go after whatever you want to do with all your might. If you're going to do something sloppy, then you might as well not do it.

Q: What would you tell an up-and-coming entrepreneur?

A: The first thing somebody needs to do when they come up with an entrepreneurial idea is question why it hasn't been done before. Then, be careful about who you talk to until you're protected. If your idea is patentable, file a provisional patent very, very quickly. Patents can cost around $15,000-$20,000, so you really need to prove the concept first. Buy some things at a hobby store and build up your experiments cheaply to prove it out.

A lot of the time the simple products are the ones that are really good. Complex products are great, but your first product needs to be simple or else you won't have the resources. Afterwards, you will have the expertise to go after a big product. But for now, go for the lowest-hanging fruit. The ideas are all there. You just have to find them.

Q: If you had to battle a giant, what weapon would you use?

A: I haven't thought about that much. Right now, my favorite pistol is a .40 caliber Glock. It's a fun little pistol. I don't think it could kill a giant, though, so maybe I would use an elephant gun.

> *Philip's Favorite Website:*
> *Google*

Q: What do you want to be when you grow up?

A: I am doing want I want to do. I'm still working on [business] and I'm not an expert at it, but I think I will be doing this for the rest of my life, possibly acting as a CEO of a company I start. I would really like to keep on setting up businesses and coming up with different business ideas. I am also looking at attending MIT in Boston, MA or the School of Mines in Golden, CO. That will be either next year or the year after that, depending on where my businesses are.

STEAM VIPER

Q: How do you plan to fund the project?

A: I have connections to a couple of different investors and I don't believe that I will have a problem getting seed funding when I am ready.

I am initially going to head towards a licensing deal. That will take anywhere from $25,000 to $150,000. I am not positive yet if I will go get investments or if I will find a way to self-fund this project.

Q: Anything else you would like to add?

A: If you love entrepreneurship, you should do it. Do what you love. But if you're not really into what you're doing, then you should go get a job and do something else. You've got to have a huge passion for it, along with a passion for helping out the world. It's not easy. If you're just doing it for the money, then it doesn't really work. You won't end up being successful.

Website: steamviper.com
Twitter: @philiphartman

> *"These interviews will bring the spirit of entrepreneurship to the world."*
>
> **~ Ysfirdaus,**
> **Comment on JuniorBiz**

PHILIP HARTMAN

*"Business is more exciting
than any game."*

- Lord Beaverbrook

4

World's Most Successful 16-Year-Old Blogger
Alex Fraiser, Blogussion
Burlington County, New Jersey

BACKGROUND

In January 2009, at the age of 15, Alex Fraiser used his web design know-how to start Blogussion.com, a blog about blogging. As the year went on, Blogussion thrived – bursting not just with insightful articles but also with an ever-growing, increasingly enthusiastic community of subscribers. In January 2010, Alex and his business partner, 24-year-old Seth Waite, launched their first product – a web theme modeled after Blogussion's unique style. It was an immediate success.

When Alex isn't helping people around the world make their blogs as popular and profitable as possible, he's just a normal high school junior in New Jersey. He lives with his family and enjoys camping, playing ping-pong, and cheering on the New England Patriots.

INTERVIEW

Q: What would you be doing right now if we weren't talking?

A: I would be blogging about blogging on Blogussion.com. We write some really in-depth content. It's on rotation with my partner, Seth. I have some posts to write this week, so I would probably be halfway through an article right now if I weren't talking to you [laughs]. It's cool. I planned ahead.

Q: What drove you above and beyond, to entrepreneurship?

A: My dad is what really inspired me to start [Blogussion.com]. He lives in Florida and owns two seafood restaurants. Obvi-

ALEX FRAISER

ously, blogging and owning a restaurant are two very different things, but the fact that he's his own boss really inspired me to go out and do it myself.

When you think of a teenager nowadays, you think of some lazy kid who has no direction in life. I don't want to be like that. I like to look deeper into things and I can't stand just sitting around. I like the idea of working hard now, so you can earn big later. I've worked in my dad's restaurants before, so I know what that's like. Manual labor sucks, dude.

Q: How do you balance your business with other priorities?

A: School has to go first. I've always been taught that if you don't succeed in school, then you're not going to succeed in life. But sometimes I think that school's maybe not what I should be focusing on the most. I'll be honest: I was so eager to develop my theme that I might have missed out on a couple of homework assignments. But if I want to keep my business going, I've got to do well in school. It's as simple as that. I love high school. I'm not about to drop out.

I've definitely been trying to balance my schoolwork and my freelancing stuff. For instance, we have all these mid-term projects for school right now. It has been crazy. But with useful productivity tips I've learned from blogging, I can manage all the different projects at once.

> *Alex's Favorite Band:*
> *Rise Against*

Q: What challenges have you faced specifically because of your age? How has your age helped you to succeed?

A: PayPal is the means to send money anywhere. Everyone uses it – but you have to be 18. I started a PayPal account on my own when I was 15. That got shut down. It stopped me from freelancing, which is what I did at the time. I couldn't pay the hosting bills for my blogs, so my blogs got stopped. It was just a huge mess that slowed me down for a couple of months. I wish that I had that time back, but it was a good lesson to learn. Now, I'm using my step-dad's account. I still don't have my own account.

My age has helped with the 'wow' factor. I love when people bring my age into it. I don't really see my age as a big issue, but other people freak out about it, so I try to use that to my advantage. Seth and I are thinking of using my age as a marketing tool. It's much easier to market yourself as a 16-year-old than as a 17-year-old, so we have to do it quick.

Q: How have people around you reacted to your success?

A: When my PayPal account got shut down, I had to go to my parents about it. At first, I was afraid they were going to say, "Whoa, no – what are you doing talking to all these creeps online?" But they completely supported me. My whole family loves it. They couldn't be more proud of me. I was completely surprised and I'm still surprised today. They think, if I'm going to be on the computer for so long, I might as well be doing something productive.

Online, they're freaking out. They love Blogussion. They love the fact that they're being preached to by this young kid. I haven't really gone to my friends and told them about everything yet. It's not really something that comes up in conversation. Maybe I'll get around to it when it's something that's earning me more serious money.

Q: How did you plan and organize your business?

A: I'm always thinking about what I can do to improve my business. I really don't like planning online or with my computer. I actually use a whiteboard. You have to keep things in your face like that. I'm thinking about getting a notebook, because I can't carry my whiteboard around. The thing is huge. Of course, you can't just plan things out; you actually have to do all the stuff you plan, too.

I'm really not a huge researcher, but you are definitely going to want to know the basics of how to start a blog. After that, I like to go with my gut feeling. It has worked out for me so far. You shouldn't always act on your first instinct, but sometimes you will get good results from it.

Q: What is the single most important reason for your success?

A: The will to keep going on. It's so easy to get unmotivated. My articles for Blogussion are huge. They take up an hour or an hour-and-a-half of my time. Sometimes I just don't feel like writing or I don't want to put in the work. But, you've got to persevere.

I started Blogussion in early 2009, when I was 15. We didn't see a penny until we launched that theme [about a year later]. You have to do more work than you will get rewarded for, especially with a blog. You can't expect to get paid on the first day. I tried selling ads for the blog when it was not ready. I only sold one or two. It was a mess. So, I don't sell ads any more.

Q: What would you tell an up-and-coming entrepreneur?

A: Always go into a new project knowing where you want to end up. I started Blogussion when I was 15; I still wanted to do it when I was 16. Now, I know I want to do it when I'm 17. Look ahead: even if your site doesn't show much promise at first, think about what it could be in three years if you keep going with it. Just look towards the future, no matter how unrealistic you make it out to be.

Generation-wide, we're the lazy teenagers. We want instant results. But nothing is instant. Don't give up so easily. Some blogs only last one or two weeks before [the writer quits] because the blog's not making millions of dollars. Come on! You've just got to give it time.

Q: If you had to battle a giant, what weapon would you use?

A: Like a cyclops giant? When I was a kid, I would go outside and my neighbors, my brother, and I would have little stick fights. I think that I'm a pretty good swordsman from that. So, I'm going to go with a sword.

I'm using my blog as a weapon to fight for success. The blog is where I go to speak, get my products out, and share all of my opinions. Without that sword, I can't beat the cyclops. Without my blog, I can't get that success.

Q: What do you want to be when you grow up?

Alex's Favorite Movie: **Step Brothers**

A: I definitely want to be my own boss. I'm loving it now. All the time I spent developing that theme, I didn't consider any of it work. All the time I was freelancing for other people, I didn't consider that work either, because I like designing websites. I definitely want to keep going with this stuff.

Everything has changed. I look back on myself before I was blogging and I was a bit lazier and not as organized. Writing a lot has really opened up my mind and allowed me to think more intellectually and deeply into subjects. Designing has really affected my life, as well. Today, I'm just a happier, better person. [My business has] opened up every possible door to a much better life.

Q: How are you going to take Blogussion to the next level?

A: My partner Seth and I have 2010 planned out: what we want to do, how we want earn, and how we want to grow our blog. Of course, nothing is guaranteed when it comes to earning income from a blog. The Blogussion theme has been such a big success for us that we have outlined our future plans around that theme and its success for our site. We are thinking about starting a whole new website that is just devoted to my Thesis skins. It has boosted our confidence. Now we

ALEX FRAISER

think that we can earn millions of dollars.

Q: What is the value of having a partner in business?

A: Blogussion has always been a joint venture. It started with another 16-year-old, but he had to go because it became too much work with school. I didn't really start to understand the value of a partnership before Seth came along. He makes the perfect sidekick because he can do what I can't do and I can do what he can't do. I rely on him so much. As we speak, he is probably writing the next great blog article for Blogussion. He's on the ball.

> **Alex's Favorite Food:**
> **Salmon**

I'm always suffering these little blogger's crashes, where I don't want to work. Sometimes I just lay down in my bed and I don't want to get up. [Having a partner] is a great motivator. Seth gets me pumped up to work.

Q: Anything else you would like to add?

A: If you want to learn more about me, check out Blogussion. It's built around my personality and my thoughts. It also has some crazy-awesome content. There's a contact form if you ever want to chat.

Website: Blogussion.com, Asnio.com
Twitter: @alexfraiser

> *"I'm a regular reader at Blogussion. Alex has done a tremendous job with his blog. When I was 16, I had never heard of blogging. I love his no ad policy. It inspired me to keep my blog ad free too. Also love his quality content. There is always something new to learn from him."*
>
> **~ Agent Deepak,**
> **Comment on JuniorBiz**

5

Rockstah Entrepreneur out of India
Farrhad Acidwalla, Rockstah Media
Mumbai, India

BACKGROUND

When Farrhad Acidwalla was in the eighth grade, his parents invested $10 so he could buy his first domain name. He began building a web community devoted to aviation and aero-modeling. The website took off and eventually Farrhad decided to move on, selling the site for far, far more than his initial $10 investment.

Since, Farrhad has launched Rockstah Media, a cutting-edge company devoted to web development, marketing, advertisement, and branding. It is just over a year old but it has clients and a full-fledged team of developers, designers and market strategists spread across the globe. As the CEO and founder, Farrhad is responsible for taking care of the clients and guiding the creative team to success.

At 16, Farrhad is planning to continue running Rockstah Media, while studying finance at India's prestigious H.R. College of Commerce & Economics. In his free time, Farrhad enjoys hanging out with friends, playing Playstation, reading, watching movies, and playing the guitar.

INTERVIEW

Q: What would you be doing right now if we weren't talking?

A: It's 7:30 pm right now, which is my time for my daily walk. Walking is my creative outlet, so that's what I would be doing right now, for the next hour-and-a-half.

Q: What drove you above and beyond, to entrepreneurship?

A: I've always had the temperament to stand aside from the crowd. My temperament isn't such that I can work under someone, unless that person has faith in my vision and appreciates my zest. So, I knew that I had to do something to stand apart and [entrepreneurship] is what I chose to do. I thought, "Ok – maybe a few websites here and there." Honestly, I didn't expect it to become this big.

My parents are very encouraging. When I first started, they really wanted me to focus on my studies. Both of them are educated and well-placed in the corporate world in India. I decided to stand apart with my own vision. They really encourage me and it's a huge asset.

> **Farrhad's Favorite TV Show:**
> **Prison Break**

I read a lot. Surfing the web, I have came across some other successful entrepreneurs – like Matthew Mullenweg, the founder of WordPress. I've read about their web startups and it has inspired me.

Q: How do you balance your business with other priorities?

A: It's a little tough, but I've managed to juggle things. I give time to my friends, working, reading, and walking. It's like an art. I've also got very understanding friends, who are really supportive. Business has never gotten in the way. I love what I do, so I don't ever worry about it or feel stress.

Q: What challenges have you faced specifically because of your age? How has your age helped you to succeed?

A: When my company wasn't known at all, I would go to a big client and they would see me and give me a look of disbelief. It was like a challenge. I would explain to them that I'm more creative and innovative because of my age, so they should look at it as an advantage. Slowly, with determination and good work, we got a couple of big clients and [the age discrimination] moved on. When they see other companies and

ROCKSTAH MEDIA

big names in my portfolio, they say, "Oh, ok – he has worked for them." Now people understand that my age is no deterrent.

Most who work with me are between the ages of 25 and 35. I was able to find these people as I was associated with them on various platforms. On spotting their like-minded attitude, I approached them to be a part of my company. My team is the backbone of the company. They give shape and form to my vision.

Q: How have people around you reacted to your success?

A: In the beginning, people were really surprised. The thing is, I never told anyone. I wanted to see how it was going to go. Then two years ago, a national paper carried an interview of mine and everybody read it. That was the turning point. Everyone was really happy for me and encouraging. I have also had a few other newspaper interviews and some very small clips on two national television programs. All these things really encourage me.

My friends are very encouraging as well. At times, they ask me if they can accompany me for a meeting. They get a lot of experience out of it and when they tell me that I've actually motivated them, it is really an amazing feeling.

Q: How did you plan and organize your business?

A: My parents offer great guidance. They always advise me to be ethical as well. Their advice on how to handle issues and the way to approach someone really helps. Work experience is something that no one can take from you. You can collect it [as a teenager] and that sure is an advantage.

[When starting Rockstah Media] I put up a website with a few developers who were all older than me. They had faith in my vision and approach. It worked out. Then, I could pay the developers and everything just fell in place.

FARRHAD ACIDWALLA

We have plans. But if anything comes, we just go and act on it. We don't think about it too much. There's no fixed long-term model or anything of the sort. We're taking one step at a time. There is no hurry; I believe in sustained and consistent growth.

Q: What is the single most important reason for your success?
A: I've never sat on an idea. If I get something, I act on it. Business is all about taking the leap. Once you take the leap, then you can think about what's going to happen next. The larger the vision, the larger the need to pave your path with skill and confidence. But, a journey of a thousand miles starts with one step. That first step is the most important thing.

> **Farrhad's Favorite Food:**
> **Indian Cuisine**

There are many in the field and each have their own ways and strategies. But one thing that I learned from my mom is to never try to copy anyone. Think of your own thing and move forward with that. Construct your own success with total confidence. I put my vision to test. I love to conceptualize, I love to illustrate, and the team's effort in creating awesomeness means a lot.

Never look left or right. Look straight at the path you have paved. Follow your vision and have your ethics in place. Yes, I get inspired by those who have had the vision – and the guts to give their vision a shape. I love to read success stories, as they teach you that failing is a part of the process and that one must not defer.

Q: What would you tell an up-and-coming entrepreneur?
A: It's never going to be easy, but you have to give it a shot or else you will regret it later. If I hadn't started my company, I would always ask, "What if it would have done well?" I would always have that regret. I really didn't want that.

Failures are the stepping stones to success. So, you have to stick to the path. You will be able to take other failures more easily, because you've had an experience with them and you know how to handle the situation now. Some young entrepreneurs don't give it enough time. Some of them don't take it seriously enough. Then they give up. I have made these mistakes and I've learned from them. I've moved on.

Q: If you had to battle a giant, what weapon would you use?

A: I couldn't really pinpoint a weapon, but I have confidence in myself and I think that's my biggest asset. That allows me to beat anyone. I'm not going to look at [the giant]. I'm just going to believe in myself and move forward. My vision and my innovative approach give me my niche.

Q: What do you want to be when you grow up?

A: Right now, I am pursuing my degree in finance and later I would like to study law. I think that these studies are going to help me with my business. But I don't think that I can have a nine-to-five job. My main goal is to be an entrepreneur.

I'm looking to continue with the same company for a while, expanding and diversifying it. My parents will keep playing an active role, as they have years of experience in their fields. Maybe one day we could create a big collaboration, but I haven't really thought too much about it. I have miles to go.

One thing that entrepreneurship has opened up for me is great exposure. I've gone to London for work and that experience was a treasure to cherish. I have been invited by a few MBA and engineering colleges to speak on my experiences in marketing and branding. Such events leave me feeling humbled and motivated. After the seminars, many have come up to me with a desire for me to help them out with their venture.

FARRHAD ACIDWALLA

Q: You have a successful and growing company, yet you've decided to stay in college. Why?

A: Education never goes to waste. Business is something that's never certain; there's always a risk. But, if you have your education in place, it's going to help you analyze challenges and deal with them. Plus, I think a few degrees to your credit sure feels good. I know there is a view that structured learning is not needed. I feel that education can never harm you and one can put it to use in more ways than one.

It's not just about making money. But while formal education will make you a living, self education will make you a fortune. If you want to really learn something and make something of yourself, self education is crucial. We learn from glory and from our own failures too.

If you learn and make efforts to manage your time properly and if you have a proper

> **Farrhad's Favorite Book:**
> **The Alchemist**
> **by Paulo Coelho**

business set up, your business can thrive while you're in college. College takes a lot of time, but I have my like-minded team who can make up for me at any given moment. My team has always supported me and my parents have always given me solid, unconditional support – and that's what I appreciate the most. I definitely haven't done all of this on my own. Today, I have a growing family across the globe and that sure means a lot.

Q: How did you find and manage your international team?

A: Through my various trips, I came across a few friends who were innovative and like-minded people. For me, that is prime. I approached them and explained my business model. They showed keen interest and I was touched by their faith in my capacity and vision. Thus, everything fell in place.

The India office was relatively easy to set up because here I

ROCKSTAH MEDIA

could search for people and meet them more easily. I mainly communicate with the ones abroad through phone calls or video conferences. In fact, we have brain-storming sessions on video conferences. Every time I conceptualize a project, I discuss the ideas, the style, and the market research. It is all very interesting. Branding, marketing – I enjoy it all.

Q: Anything else you would like to add?
A: For young entrepreneurs, I would say one thing: even if you get success early, it shouldn't intoxicate you. There are miles to go. There are lots of things to do in life. You need to diversify and innovate all the time. You shouldn't lose focus and get intoxicated with success.

Website: RockstahMedia.com, LetsSermo.com
Twitter: @farrhad

> *"Certainly amongst the brightest and the most talented teenagers I have ever met. Not to forget the golden heart as well!"*
>
> **~ Annkur,**
> **Comment on JuniorBiz**

FARRHAD ACIDWALLA

"Not tomorrow. Not next week. But today.
The true entrepreneur is a doer,
not a dreamer."

- Nolan Bushnell

6

11 Companies and 3 Foundations by Age 17
Mark Bao, Avecora
Boston, Massachusetts

BACKGROUND

Mark Bao had his first encounter with entrepreneurship in the fifth grade. He used Visual Basic 6.0 to write a simple computer application that managed his homework assignments and helped him write school papers. Then he copied the program onto floppy discs and sold them to his friends.

His first start-up came in his first year of high school. Debateware.com was an event management system for debate organizations. Eventually, Mark and his business partner sold it to the largest debate organization in the United States.

Today, Mark is a 17-year-old high school senior and he has already launched 11 web-based companies (selling three of them) along with three non-profit foundations. Some of his projects include TickrTalk, the Ramamia Foundation, Classleaf, and Avecora – a technology network launching sometime in 2013.

INTERVIEW

Q: What would you be doing right now if we weren't talking?

A: Right now, I would be working. I was actually on a conference call before [this interview]. I'm working on launching a start-up called Genevine, which is a website where families can privately share photos, events, and messages. We're raising funding for it from angel investors, so we're preparing our documents for that.

Q: What drove you above and beyond, to entrepreneurship?

A: With my first start-up, DebateWare.com, it was just about getting some money to save up for college. After a few years, I started to realize what entrepreneurship is really about. For me at least, it's about making a change in the technology sector and in the world as a whole. My personal life goal is to make people smile a little bit more. I hope my companies will help create value and make people happier in the long run. That's what I'm in it for.

I highly recommend *The Art of the Start* by Guy Kawasaki and *Founders at Work* by Jessica Livingston. For young entrepreneurship, I would recommend *My Start-up Life* by Ben Casnocha and *Zero to One Million* by Ryan P. Allis.

Q: How do you balance your business with other priorities?

A: In the past few years, I have mostly been focused on business. I work about 60 hours a week or more. The balance has come from a vigorous work strategy: I try to make every hour count whenever I work on anything. Every hour has a purpose. But this has kind of made me not enjoy life as much.

> *Mark's Favorite Website:*
> *Facebook*

In the last few months, my senior year, I have realized that I won't get childhood again and I should enjoy it a little bit more. I also have to worry about school and homework more, since my grades are affecting what college I can get into and whatnot.

Q: What challenges have you faced specifically because of your age? How has your age helped you to succeed?

A: The number one challenge I've seen with myself and with other teen entrepreneurs is that they get too caught up in the idea that teen entrepreneurs are supposed to be cut some slack for what they do. That mindset undermines your potential. I just try to think of myself as an entrepreneur who happens to be a teen.

On the other side, [my age] has gotten me press, which is nice. I've been invited to speak about Generation Y at Gnomedex and about teen entrepreneurs at TYE in Boston.

Q: How have people around you reacted to your success?

A: The main thing that people ask is, "How do you find the time to do all this?" It has made a name for me in school as the guy who does business. It's kind of annoying because some people don't talk to me as much because they think I'm always busy or something. But the most common response is just, "Wow – that's cool."

Q: How did you plan and organize your business?

A: I create a roadmap for every month. It's a document that states the main tasks that I need to do for the next month. I don't keep this on the computer. I print it out and I keep it inside a folder with all of my project stuff. It's a living document because I can keep writing on it, circling what I need to do. Even though it's a simple idea, it has proven really effective for me.

> *Mark's Favorite Book:*
> **Tuesdays with Morrie**
> *by Mitch Albom*

For young entrepreneurs, I think it's a good idea to put together a checklist for starting a business. Have one page for each section, like accounting and your business plan. That way, you can see what type of work you're getting into and what you need to do.

Q: What is the single most important reason for your success?

A: My main goal is to create value for the customer. One of the ways I'm doing that is with Genevine. We're helping families keep in touch with each other. We've created value for these families because we've centralized everything in one place for them and we have a really simple service that they can use. We've gotten so many emails from people who say,

MARK BAO

"Thank you so much for creating this product. It helps to keep our family together." That really keeps me going: praise from the customers and the idea that I am helping people enjoy life a little bit more.

Q: If you had to battle a giant, what weapon would you use?
A: I don't know. Probably a bunch of lawyers... with swords.

Q: What do you want to be when you grow up?
A: I still want to do entrepreneurship. Avecora is helping people communicate better and experience technology in a new way. That's the company that I want to build an empire out of.

> **Mark's Favorite Band:**
> **A Fine Frenzy**

We're always working on the non-profits as well. My preliminary life goal is to donate 80% to humanitarian aid and research. Since my career goal is to earn $10 billion, that would be $8 billion. Another 10% will go to The Mark Bao Foundation, where we manage research grants and lobby for better funding for NASA and the National Institute of Health (NIH). Another 5% will go to funding start-ups, helping them grow.

Q: Why is philanthropy so important to you?
A: The Ramamia Foundation started when there was a Twitter fundraiser for a single mother who was evicted from her household. It was raising money for her to keep going and pay rent. We thought that giving back to the society as a whole was something that all entrepreneurs should be part of. While you do give value through your product, you can create more value by giving back as well.

Q: You've created 11 web-based companies and you've sold three of them. What is it like to sell one of your companies?
A: The buyers mostly just come to us. They recognize our company, make an offer and, in some cases, we go ahead with

AVECORA

it. The problem with a lot of start-ups is that they try to go for an acquisition [from the onset] and they don't focus as much on the money-making part of it. That's why most of my companies focus on making money, not hoping for an acquisition.

Part of my struggle is that I want to see where the buyers are going with the business and, in most cases, I don't have control over that. Like with a baby, I just want to make sure that it's going to have a good future – and that the new caretakers will promote the ideas on which I founded the company.

Q: Anything else you would like to add?
A: I just want people to create companies that are awesome, create value, and give back to the community as a whole. I really hope they do.

Website: MarkBao.com, Branchr.com
Twitter: @markbao

MARK BAO

"It's always great to see an entrepreneur who has passion for what he does and who knows exactly what he wants. It's crucial to set high goals in life and business and more importantly give back to the community. Nice job!"

**~ Euveshan G,
Comment on JuniorBiz**

Editor's Note: Since this interview, Mark Bao has become the CTO of Branchr Advertising, with Christian Owens.

*"A ship in harbor is safe,
but that is not what ships are built for."*

- William Shedd

7

World's Youngest Best-Selling Author
Stanley Tang, Author of *eMillions*
Hong Kong

BACKGROUND

When Stanley Tang was an 11-year-old growing up in Hong Kong, his school banned snack foods. Instead of taking his empty stomach in stride, Stanley bought snacks at the local convenience store and sold them to his classmates for three times the price. A few years later, he was introduced to Google Adsense and the *Rich Dad, Poor Dad* series of books by Robert Kiyosaki. They inspired him to get online with his business and to develop a book called *eMillions: Behind-The-Scenes Stories of 14 Successful Internet Millionaires*.

When *eMillions* was published in December of 2008, it rocketed straight to the top of the Amazon Best-Seller lists. At just 14 years old, Stanley was the world's youngest best-selling author. Since, he has been making six figures with his blogs, StanleyTang.com and TheUniversityKid.com, which he eventually sold to another young entrepreneur. Now 17, Stanley just graduated high school in May of 2010 and he will be attending Stanford University in the fall, where he plans to study something in computer science.

INTERVIEW

Q: What would you be doing right now if we weren't talking?

A: I just graduated high school, so I would probably just be relaxing and getting ready for summer. At the same time, I would probably be learning some programming: playing around with php, java script, and some more advanced stuff.

Q: What drove you above and beyond, to entrepreneurship?

A: I've always been pretty passionate about entrepreneurship. When I was 11, my school banned snacks. So, I brought snacks from home and sold them at school for three times the price. That made me enough for pocket money, to buy extra junk.

> **Stanley's Favorite Food: Chicken Wings**

In 2005, I came across a book, *Rich Dad Poor Dad* by Robert Kiyosaki. That book was pretty inspirational and vital to my success. It introduced me to the business world in basic and fundamental terms. Soon after, I read other business books and I came across Google Adsense in 2006. That's how I got started.

Q: How do you balance your business with other priorities?

A: To be honest, I don't think that you can efficiently balance school and business at the same time. It has to be one or the other. If you try to balance both, you end up doing a mediocre job on both. When I wrote *eMillions*, I focused a lot on my business and my grades kind of suffered.

When I interviewed Jeremy Shoemaker from Shoemoney, the interview was at eight o'clock in the morning on a school day. I had a choice to either skip school or give up on the interview. High school was less precious, so I chose business.

My parents were pretty supportive, but they warned me, "Don't let your grades slip too much." I stayed up until 1:00 or 2:00 am, so I had little sleep and little time to do homework. When I finished *eMillions*, I took a hiatus from my business and focused on my grades to get into a university.

Q: What challenges have you faced specifically because of your age? How has your age helped you to succeed?

A: There are obviously legal issues: things like assets, PayPal, and taxes. So you have to make that sure that you have your parents' support. As a young entrepreneur, it's also pretty difficult to make connections with older entrepreneurs. Many are reluctant to do business with you once they find out that you're just 13 or 14.

Networking might be difficult, but a lot of other entrepreneurs got really inspired and motivated when I told them my age. They wanted to help me even more because of the fact that I was just getting started. At the same time, your age is a unique selling point. It's a way to differentiate you from other people. You can build a great story around your age, generate huge buzz, and attract the press. The press loves stories about young entrepreneurs.

Q: How have people around you reacted to your success?
A: My family and friends are really proud of my success. My family is 100% behind me pursuing entrepreneurship and that's a huge key to my success. Make sure that you have the full support of your family. Otherwise, it will be extremely difficult to deal with many of the challenges, emotionally and legally. I have friends who started with entrepreneurship and their parents were 100% against them. Now, they're finding it difficult to go through the whole process.

[On being featured in Mexico's GQ Magazine] GQ had seen my book project emails and they happened to have a contact who had also seen my project. Honestly, I had no idea they were going to feature me on a homepage or front cover. I thought that I would be in some small corner at the bottom. I got a lot of Twitter messages from people in Mexico and Latin America. So, I attracted a new audience for my blog.

I've gotten a lot of responses from relatives who I barely knew, like my fifth cousin. I had to ask my mom, "Who are these people?" I have met a lot of new relatives. So that's pretty cool.

Q: How did you plan and organize your business?

A: I'm more of a spontaneous person. I tend to do things in short, efficient bursts, rather than spreading them out. It's a personal preference. I tried the whole planning thing with *eMillions*, but I quickly found out that it just didn't work for me. As soon as one schedule went off track, the whole plan basically stopped.

So, I try to keep my planning simple. I just use a basic to-do list. I send an email to myself with all of the bullet points, so that I can access it from anywhere in the world. When I accomplish something, I cross it off. This list guides what I need to do to keep me on track.

Q: What is the single most important reason for your success?

A: It comes down to hard work. There is no magic pill to get overnight success. Overnight success doesn't exist. *eMillions* took 15 months. But, then it seemed like it came out of nowhere when the book launched.

Success comes down to hard work plus passion, over time. If you work really, re-

> *Stanley's Favorite Movie:*
> **The Dark Knight**

ally hard over a long period of time, it will pay off. It's not about working super-hard for a week and then expecting a huge payload. For example, when you tried to arrange this interview for me, you were really persistent. That is what I admired about you.

Q: What would you tell an up-and-coming entrepreneur?

A: Constantly tweak your business. I think too many entrepreneurs try to be a perfectionist and then all they do is plan, plan, talk, and plan some more. In the end, they get nothing done. What you finish with is probably going to be completely different than what you initially started with, anyway. So, I think that you just need to go out there and experiment. You have to take action.

You also have to stay grounded and humble. A lot of times when young entrepreneurs find success, they suddenly think that they're the most successful person in the world. Sometimes they get too cocky and go off-track. Keep your feet grounded.

Q: If you had to battle a giant, what weapon would you use?
A: I'm going to cheat and say that I would use my brains. You always have to be analyzing and assessing whether or not things are working out. You also have to understand that you can't do it all by yourself. Business is a team project. It may seem like *eMillions* was just me, but I actually had a transcriptionist, a mentor, a graphic designer, and a copywriter.

Q: What do you want to be when you grow up?
A: I've been taking a break from my internet business over the past six months. After reflecting, I'm probably not going to continue to pursue internet/information marketing (like eBooks). I will probably focus more towards technology-oriented startup businesses. A lot of those internet marketing concepts still apply, such as web 2.0 sites, conversion rates, and copywriting. So, I'll still be using my experience.

Internet marketing is what gave me the opportunity to get into Stanford. Not a lot of 17-year-old seniors applying to Stanford own a full internet business. So the admissions officers might have seen that and been impressed. My grades aren't Ivy League grades, so I think that is what really got me into Stanford.

I will see what opportunities there are in Silicon Valley. Mobile is pretty hot right now; location-based services and real-time services are pretty hot right now. Maybe I'll get a job and get some experience first and we'll see how things go from there.

STANLEY TANG

Q: How did you make *eMillions* an instant #1 best-seller?

A: Basically, you have to coordinate a successful product launch. I sent out a blog post, wrote tweets, and all of that stuff. But, you also have to have a great sales letter that converts and an irresistible offer. When *eMillions* came out, I said, "Buy this book – and I'll give you all of these great bonuses."

> **Stanley's Favorite TV Show:**
> **Survivor**

The bonuses came from my affiliate and joint venture partners, who also promoted the book on the same day and sent out an email to their list. Obviously, you first have to gather and contact all of those partners. For *eMillions*, naturally, the joint venture partners were the 14 internet entrepreneurs who I interviewed. Since they were part of the book, they wanted to promote the book – a win-win situation.

I think the press was a huge factor as well. I got featured on the front page of the second largest newspaper in Hong Kong. That attracted a huge buzz. I think I got something like 15,000 unique visitors in 24 hours to my website, Stanley-Tang.com. It actually crashed on the day I was featured.

Writing a book is not for the money. You could make way more money if you simply repurposed that content as a video course or anything like that. You could sell it for $99 or $199, rather than just $20. But writing a book is not just about the money; it's about all of the benefits that come with the book, like credibility. So, even though Amazon takes a huge chunk and my publisher takes a huge chunk, I think that it is a great platform to distribute your book. It's more about getting to a wider audience, as opposed to just making money.

Q: You have over 100,000 followers on Twitter. How did you manage to build such a gigantic community?

A: I promoted my Twitter a lot last year. I sent out emails to my lists, saying, "Follow me on Twitter." Back then, Twitter was the thing that everybody was talking about. I engaged a lot with my followers. Whenever people talked to me, I would always reply. That helps you build a huge Twitter following.

Over the past year, the effectiveness of Twitter as a marketing tool has decreased slightly. Before, when I had 10,000 followers and I sent out a link, I'd probably get the same amount of clicks as I get today – and I have over 100,000 followers. Twitter has gotten kind of saturated.

I would start with Facebook, as opposed to Twitter. Mark Zuckerberg has done some amazing things, including the open graph project, which is a great idea to connect people. Facebook is going to be the next Google.

Q: What do you see as the power of an interview?

A: You can learn a lot about the person you are interviewing through their story and their mindset of success. They can be great people to model yourself after. Secondly, you can publish your interviews online and be an expert by association. You're interviewing all of the experts in your niche, so you become an expert yourself.

One difficulty is that interviewing is pretty time-consuming. It takes a lot of effort to get the person to agree to interview. Some people will reject your interview proposal. Hong Kong is halfway around the world, so the time zone is a big issue. A lot of my interviews happened at two o'clock in the morning. It's definitely easier said than done.

Q: Anything else you would like to add?

A: To all of the young entrepreneurs out there, just go out there and take action. Take a risk. Follow your passion. The best

STANLEY TANG

time to take action is when you're a teenager. You've got nothing to lose. If your business fails, so what? You've always got your parents and your school to fall back on. Later in life, it's going to be harder because you will have responsibilities, like a family. Now is the best time to take action.

Website: StanleyTang.com, eMillionsBook.com
Twitter: @stanleytang

"It inspires me when I see young people doing great in business. This tells me that there is nobody that cannot make it in life or business. There are two things you need to excel in and that is what Stanley Tang displays: (1) The ability to recognize opportunities, (2) The courage to pursue those opportunities. Let's make the most of every opportunity that shows up on our path. Make the world proud! Make Nick Scheidies and Nick Tart proud and make yourself proud too!"

~ Seun K,
Comment on JuniorBiz

AUTHOR OF *eMILLIONS*

8

Dude with Two Six-Figure Products
Adam Horwitz, Adasim Inc.
Los Angeles, California

BACKGROUND
When Adam Horwitz was a 15-year-old high school sophomore growing up in the Pacific Palisades, a mean-spirited gossip blog caught fire with his classmates. Concerned parents soon stomped it out, but Adam's newfound desire to find online success would prove much harder to extinguish.

He started Urban Stomp, a website where he posted music and the locations of parties in the area. The site made a profit by selling clothes through affiliate links. Adam proved too success-ful for his own good: Urban Stomp drove 800 people to one party. He had to shut it down after only a few weeks.

Adam has learned from his mistakes and now teaches people age 15 and older how to make money online. He practices what he preaches: his courses, *Tycoon Cash Flow* and *Cell Phone Treasure*, have each earned over $100,000 and he has another one in the works, called *Dude I Hate My Job*. To get his blood flowing, Adam enjoys driving his newly-purchased 2010 Audi A5 and playing *Call of Duty: Modern Warfare 2* on his Xbox 360.

INTERVIEW
Q: What would you be doing right now if we weren't talking?
A: I would be working on my courses. At the moment, I have a new course coming out called *Dude I Hate My Job*, so I'm trying to put all of this stuff together for that. I'm just gener-ating all of the videos and all of the content. It's a lot of work

up front, but once it's done, it will be on auto-pilot. Hopefully, that will be released in the next month. I don't have an exact launch date yet.

Q: What drove you above and beyond, to entrepreneurship?

A: All of my friends were doing babysitting jobs. I wanted money without the job. As soon as I saw a blog pop up at my school that became this huge thing, I decided that there must be something there.

Adam's Favorite TV Show:
Entourage

So, I started up a party website where I posted parties in Los Angeles. It immediately got shut down after about 800 kids showed up at a house. I didn't know the party was cancelled. It was a huge mix-up. So I had to stop that. That's when I was in tenth grade. All of my friends thought I was crazy, trust me. And it took me two years, testing things out. I just kept going at it, determined to do it, and – finally – I hit it. It was a fun experience all the way up.

I think that I just have a lot of determination inside of me. It's weird. I focused on [my online businesses] 24/7. Right when I got back from school, it was all I would do. Even though this sounds ridiculous, I would drive past big homes and just stare at them. It was to get in the right mindset, to think, "That's where I will be living some day."

Q: How do you balance your business with other priorities?

A: Right now, I'm taking a semester off of college because my business has really picked up. I'm going back, but in high school, I was never really into school. I got B's, passed the classes, and graduated high school with no questions – but I just took the easy way out. I never took the really challenging courses or anything. I pretty much took what I needed to take, got my diploma, and that was that.

ADASIM INC.

Mondays through Thursdays were my workdays. The week-ends I would be with my friends. Then school would be in the mornings. That's how I did it. It balanced it out. Senior year, I made sure that I got out of class every day at 11:00 am. I messed with my schedule so that I could go straight home and start working.

The great thing about the internet is that you don't even have to have a high school degree. As long as you are dedi-cated, you can start up your own business. 20 years ago, that wasn't possible. You had to have so much money up front. But now, you can go and start up a Facebook fan page or a YouTube channel. YouTube will actually pay you money to put up videos of you doing diddly-squat. It's a whole new generation and anyone can do that with just a little video camera.

Q: What challenges have you faced specifically because of your age? How has your age helped you to succeed?

A: People didn't believe me at first. Even my friends were so stereotyped into thinking that you can't do anything when you're young – that you have to wait until you're older and have a degree to actually become successful. So, whenever I would tell people, "I'm doing this," they wouldn't take it seri-ously. Now that I have my Audi A5, everyone's jumping on the bandwagon.

Age also has its benefits. For instance, I use my age as a mar-keting advantage. I can target younger people. I'm 18 years old. I say, "If I'm 18 years old, you could be doing the same thing no matter how old you are."

When you're young, what do you have to lose? You're still living at home. You don't have 50 bills you have to cover. All you've got to do is cover your late night dinners and your pizzas and all that. If everything completely fails, you're still at school. You're still going to get your degree. So, it doesn't

Adam Horwitz

matter as long as you have fun doing it. Work your way up and stay dedicated. There's no real loss. Enjoy the way up.

I'm living at home still. I don't have to pay for rent or anything, so I can just put it in the bank. That's really a big benefit: building up equity. Stay at home as long as you possibly can, even if you're making a lot of money. Don't stay until you're 30, though [laughs]. And if you're 60: you've got to be out.

Q: How have people around you reacted to your success?
A: Now that I have the car, people say, "Whoa! Show me how to do it!" Before, they would just say, "That's cool Adam. Go do your thing," – even though it was the exact same ink (money) that I was making a month ago. Now, all of a sudden, they want to get on it and try it themselves.

My family has always been there for me and they've always said that I could do it. Now that I've

> **Adam's Favorite Book:**
> **Crush It**
> *by Gary Vaynerchuk*

got this far, they're very happy for me. So, that's good. In the beginning, they were like "Do you really need [an Audi A5]?" But they are happy for me now that I have it. They're from a generation where, when you were this age, you didn't even have a car. You had to take the bus, take the train, or ride a zebra [laughs]. They're from South Africa, so it's a whole different mindset.

Q: How did you plan and organize your business?
A: I didn't really plan or organize anything. I just said, "All right – this is where I want to get to." Then I kept trying things until I got to that point. I'm bad at organizing, but I have good memory. So I just kept all of it running in my brain.

Setting goals is really important. On top of my bed, whenever I went to sleep, I'd read my goal. It was to make a million

ADASIM INC.

dollars by 21. I may have to update my goal, though. I set it when I was 15.

Q: What is the single most important reason for your success?

A: Dedication. The hardest part about being an entrepreneur is that you'll fail ten times for every success. So, I've failed at least 30 times with different websites and stuff. I've tried everything. I tried to set up a social media site about skateboarding tricks. And [Urban Stomp] failed after the cops had to talk to me. But, they were not failures to me. They just didn't work – and if I hadn't failed all of those times, I wouldn't be where I'm at now.

A lot of my friends see that I'm successful now, but they don't see all of the failures from before. They think that if they just start now, they are instantly going to become successful. The same with the courses: I teach people how to get started online. But they think that once they join the course, they're going to be millionaires the next day. I'll guide you to that point, but you have to work. You can't just sit there, open up your account, go play some videogames, and come back thinking that you're going to have $100 in your account. It's not going to work. You can't just snap your fingers and have money fall out of the sky. I wish. If that was the case, I would be driving a Bugatti right now, living like a king in a castle [laughs].

Q: What would you tell an up-and-coming entrepreneur?

A: Even if you fail the first time, who cares? What's going to happen? You're young. The worst thing that could happen to you is that you wake up and go to school the next day. So just keep at whatever you're doing and I promise you you'll hit it. It's all about perseverance.

Entrepreneurs have this thing inside of them where they don't necessarily give up very easily. But people have the mindset from the media that they can get rich overnight. It's

Adam Horwitz

possible to do anything, but you have to keep working at it. If you give up, then what's going to happen? You're just going to sit there and wonder what would have happened a year down the road if you had kept doing it.

Maybe the idea you had will have been taken by another entrepreneur. I think it has been proven that whenever you have a really good idea, there are at least three or four people in the world that have the exact same idea at the exact same time as you. There are a lot of entrepreneurs out there. So, if you're not going to do it, they're going to do it.

Q: If you had to battle a giant, what weapon would you use?

A: I'm sure some people would say, "Pull out a bazooka." But, no matter what my weapon was, it would be my dedication, motivation, and perseverance that would take the giant down. I don't need a weapon to do it as long as I believe that I'm going to. I could win the battle with a stick – as long as I stand there whacking the giant with it for the next 72 hours.

> **Adam's Favorite Band:**
> **Lil Wayne**

Like I've been saying: just don't give up. It's the number one way that I see people mess up in this business. They try their hardest for three weeks and then, if they see nothing, it's over. They think it's the end of the world. It's never going to work. So they just start something new. It's an ongoing cycle. They do that again and again and they never sit down and actually do anything.

Q: What do you want to be when you grow up?

A: I want to keep doing what I'm doing, but I want to own a much bigger business online. It might not be in courses. It may be a service of some sort or a social networking site, but I would like to have a few income streams. Eventually, I want to use the money that I make to invest in real estate and spread my wings everywhere instead of putting everything in one basket.

Q: How did you build a list of 150,000 potential customers?

A: I started collecting emails from my party site. They were pretty much my friends' emails, because they were all at my school. Now, before anyone can get to the next page for one of my courses, they have to fill in their name and email. I get a lot of name and emails from that, just from my courses becoming so popular. One of my courses became one of the top 100 products on ClickBank within the first three months – and ClickBank has over 10,000 products. By traffic, my best day was when 75,000 people visited my site. So, I have some days where I get over 1,000 people filling in their name and email.

> **Adam's Favorite Website:**
> **Facebook**

Building a list is huge. I'm telling you now, it's the future. Any offline business has so much more potential once it goes online. No matter what, even if your website goes down, you always have that list. You can always talk to those people, send them information, and send them courses. As long as you keep a good relationship with your list, there will always be people buying. It's pretty much like having a virtual ATM.

I would have to say 30-50% have become repeat customers. If I deliver good content and it helps them make money, then why wouldn't they spend the money that they made out of my previous courses on more courses for me? For these types of courses, they're not just spending their money. They're *investing* their money. Some guy actually said, "Just because you made us this much money from your last course, I'm buying all of your courses from now on. Even if I don't use them, I'm just going to buy them to support you." I was like "Yeah! That's great, dude. Go for it!" When you help people, they're just so generous.

ADAM HORWITZ

Q: How has featuring your personality through video helped your business?

A: All of my courses are video. I'm not into having the written stuff. I like the video for the younger people who want to get started online. They want to just kick back with a Coke or something and watch how to do it. So, when people come to my sales page, they don't want to have to read a bunch of stuff to figure out what it's all about. My video will pop up and I will literally talk to them like I'm talking to you. I can connect with people with my personality and all of my customers feel like they're my friends. That's a huge part of it: if you can make a customer feel comfortable with you and feel like they can talk to you whenever they want, then you're going to be successful no matter what.

Q: Anything else you would like to add?

A: Don't listen to what other people say. If you're a young entrepreneur and you're trying to make it big online, don't think that you can't do it. With the internet the way it is now, you can do anything. Even if everyone is saying, "No – it will never happen. Everything online is a scam!" Honestly: just screw them. Check them out of your mind and go for it. That's what I did and I'm doing well, I think.

Website: AdamHorwitz.tv
Twitter: @adamhorwitz

> *"An E-Course can be an awesome earner. It takes a few years to establish a brand and have an authoritative website. If you blog consistently for 5 years around a subject then the sky is the limit for traffic, advertising revenue and click bank sales! I just wished I started at 15, at the age of 20 I could have been a millionaire!"*
>
> **~ David E,**
> **Comment on JuniorBiz**

9

The Outlaw Entrepreneur
King Sidharth, Createens
Chandigarh, India

BACKGROUND

As an 11-year-old growing up in a backward sector of Northern India, King Sidharth and a few friends began organizing events and competitions for other children. They would make tickets and charge an entry fee, then award little prizes to whoever won. In an area where there wasn't much else to do, Sidharth's first business was a big success.

Now 18, King Sidharth has just graduated from high school and he has already made a name for himself as one of India's top young entrepreneurs. His primary work is in website development and design, but – like many young entrepreneurs – he's never content working on just one thing.

King is also a speaker on topics of entrepreneurship and spirituality. He's currently writing an e-magazine for teens (*FRiEnDz*) and a book about the intersection of spirituality and science (*Bhagvad Gita & the Law of Attraction*). He's also developing a movie that peeks into the lives of some young entrepreneurs (*FRiEnDz: The Movie*). Lastly, King is organizing a conference for teenagers called Createens. It will give young people an opportunity to learn about entrepreneurship, blogging, and more from worldwide experts.

INTERVIEW

Q: What would you be doing right now if we weren't talking?

A: I'd be working on my book, writing about bridging spirituality and science. Or maybe I would just be sleeping. But it would be one of those two things.

Q: What drove you above and beyond, to entrepreneurship?

A: The biggest influence in my life for [entrepreneurship] was my father. When I was ten, he was trying to set up his own business. I saw that he would rather earn less and do what he loves than earn ten times more and do another's bidding. I felt the same way. Spiritual books all talk to you about the same issue: no person other than you is worth following. That's what inspired me to take on my own inner calling.

I realized that I cannot work for anyone. I cannot take orders. I would rather do something for free for myself than earn money and feel that I'm working for someone else. I just love my freedom too much. I want to wake when I want, sleep when I want, eat when I want, and I figured out that entrepreneurship is the best way to do that. If you can do things that you love doing and you can make money out of it, then it's a done deal. It's the best life you could ever have.

Q: How do you balance your business with other priorities?

A: I never realize that I am balancing at all. When you do the stuff that you love, then timing goes out of the equation. Your timing is perfect. When your school, friends, and family see the lifestyle you are enjoying and how good you feel in doing that, then they start spoiling you after a while. My school would excuse me for a whole month so that I could work on one of my projects. If I go to the city and I need to meet someone for a project, I could stay at [a friend's] place. All you have to do is follow your passion; everything else will fall into place.

Recently, my high school final exams were going on, which will stick with me for my whole life. But I couldn't get off of Twitter; I couldn't get off of email; I couldn't distract myself from all of the business stuff and get to the books. I realized that since I was happy doing these things, then I would go to my books more happily. Life needs to be attended happily and positively. So, your passion cannot hurt anything else. It cannot. You cannot follow your passion and let bad things happen in life.

Q: **What challenges have you faced specifically because of your age? How has your age helped you to succeed?**

A: The only thing that didn't work out because of my age was when a group of university students in my home town were setting up something big. They needed someone who could give a talk on entrepreneurship and spirituality. I was recommended to them by a friend of mine and they wanted to meet me. I went there and they saw that I was 16 years old. They didn't give me a chance.

> **King's Favorite TV Show:**
> **Dr. Who**

In other ways, it has been a great advantage. People see the passion in me and they say, "This is someone I want to work with." As you get older, people start believing less and less in themselves. They're not as passionate. But you want to work with people who can spend nights and nights without sleep because they're so passionate. Being young, I can do that.

All of the elders are convinced that they are the ones who know how to live. But the people who are successes never followed the ways that their parents were trying to teach them. Can you imagine how Bill Gates' parents reacted when he told them that he was going to drop out of his university? They must have freaked out. They want you to play it safe. They don't want you to get hurt. But if you're not doing the things that you love, then your life is not worth living. What are you here for?

I can guarantee that if you do stuff you love, then money

KING SIDHARTH

will fall into place. You'll never have to worry about money. You can kill me if that doesn't happen. Jesus said, "Do birds ever worry? Do they ever sow? Do they ever reap?" No, they don't worry about that [and all of their needs are accounted for]. Why wouldn't the heavenly father do the same for us? That's the basis of enterprising (entrepreneurship): do the stuff you love and everything falls into place.

Q: How have people around you reacted to your success?

A: First of all, my father was always supportive. He always takes risks and he loves for me to take risks too. He doesn't interfere. But for every entrepreneur out there, people are going to freak out a bit when you first start. Your parents and your friends are going to think that you've totally lost it. "You need a psychiatrist." But later, when you're successful, they're going to support you. People in my family are now funding my stuff.

> **King's Favorite Food: Cheese**

So, don't look for support from outside of you. Look for support in how you feel about what you're doing. The major difference between an entrepreneur and anybody else is that an entrepreneur sees an outcome before it comes. You know it's going to happen. But others can't see it. That's what Jesus is talking about when he says, "Blessed are those who believe without seeing." They are the people who are going to thrive in this world. So, as an entrepreneur, you have got to believe in your gut feeling. Other people may or may not believe it.

Q: How did you plan and organize your business?

A: I didn't realize I was doing business. I just followed my inner calling. The best thing that I've done is to never follow anyone's advice. If I wanted to publish a blog, I wouldn't follow anyone's advice. I would research on my own, find Word-Press, and follow my gut. So, my planning was more from experience in real life.

You don't have to go out and look for tools and advice. When you look at it as a goal, instead of a problem, the answers will come right on your doorstep. It was just one year ago that I realized that what I was doing was entrepreneurship. Just two weeks ago, I learned how to spell it [laughs].

Q: What is the single most important reason for your success?

A: I keep everybody out of the equation and follow my own inner calling. A lot of people get caught up asking, "What do you think, mother of mine? What do you think, father of mine?" But there are a thousand different people and you're going to get a thousand different responses: somebody pointing you South, ten people pointing you North, even more pointing East. Where are you going to go? Go with yourself. Your point of view is unique in the world.

When you're done with your vision, then you might ask for advice on minor things. You have to strike a balance. But even after asking people, follow what you think out of it, not what they think. Take Google and Yahoo. These two are different perspectives of solving the same problem: finding content on the internet. Yahoo keeps on listening to people. Google doesn't care. They never ask you what their home page should look like. They never ask you anything – and that is really behind their success. They do it themselves. Then later, they might ask you how they could improve it.

Q: What would you tell an up-and-coming entrepreneur?

A: The best advice I would give to them is to just get started. There will be a lot of unanswered questions. How are you going to get started? How is income going to come? What system are you going to use? These are irrelevant. There's only one question that matters: what do you want to do?

The information age is growing. There's no lack of information, but there always will be a lack of new ideas. So the most important thing is your idea, your business. Do something, maybe just one step. Write it down, draw a diagram, write a blog post, or talk to someone about it – but just get started. Take a baby-step forward and you just moved towards becoming a successful entrepreneur.

The funny thing is that the ideas are not yours. They're in the common conscious. But how you perceive an idea is yours. It's unique to you. Google wasn't the first search engine, but how they perceived the idea was unique. One of my friends was thinking about writing a book. I said, "You have a laptop. You have a word processor. Just start writing!" But, he was still attending to the unanswered questions. The next thing he knew, one week later, a book came out that was talking about exactly the same thing he was talking about. That's how the universe works. The universe gives an idea to you because the universe thinks you're the best person to take care of it. But if you are not acting, it goes to another person.

Even if someone has stolen that idea, so to speak, you can still pursue it and be successful. Facebook and Google were not the first in the field, but they definitely are the best in their fields. But you don't even have to do it better: you just have to do it your way. Crystals of ice are always unique in shape, size, and formation. There's never the same ice crystal. There's never the same DNA. When you are unique, there is no competition.

Q: If you had to battle a giant, what weapon would you use?
A: I am going to be a bit philosophical. Now, there is no way that I can battle a giant with physical effort. I'm like an ant that he could just crush under his thumb. The easiest way to battle anything or anyone in life – which I take from Jesus Christ, Buddha, Abraham Hicks, and every great person in this world – is to turn the other cheek. That doesn't just mean that if someone slaps you on one side of the face, then you offer the other. It means, you *look* in the other direction.

You change. Jesus and Buddha were living guarantees that, if your consciousness changes, your reality changes too.

When you shift your consciousness so that you don't perceive the giant as an enemy, you don't need to battle anymore. You can be friends with the giant – and how good it is to be friends with a giant? Now you can have much more influence. You can get things done that you couldn't have done earlier because you can bully people now. Everybody knows that they would much rather have a friend than an enemy. Now, I have a friend called 'Giant'.

Q: What do you want to be when you grow up?
A: This question has been asked a lot recently, because my high school has ended. What I want to be when I grow up is a happy person. That's all. I want to be a person who does what he loves and loves what he does and in doing that, he uplifts everyone else. I'm doing it already, at some level of my being.

> **King's Favorite Book:**
> **Ask and It Is Given**
> **by Esther & Jerry Hicks**

As children, we tend to switch so frequently what we want to become. "Today, I want to be a milkman because I love the milk he sells. Tomorrow, I want to be a sweets seller because I love the sweets he sells." It keeps on changing, doesn't it? But people say you should decide one thing. I don't think I could be doing one thing for the rest of my life and be happy in it. Impossible!

I can't be writing for Meditation Rocks for the rest of my life and be happy about it, no matter how much it's paying me. I want to follow what my life puts out in front of me and follow my inner calling. When I do that, uplifting others will fall into place automatically.

KING SIDHARTH

Q: Where does your enthusiasm come from and why is it important?

A: My enthusiasm comes from alignment. Alignment means being happy no matter what and believing in yourself no matter what. The basic premise of my living is that I am going to be happy. I start off my day with that. That means that I am going to believe in myself no matter what, because if I believe in myself, then I can handle anything that life throws at me. And that makes me happy.

The enthusiasm comes from knowing that all is well and that everything is going to fall into place. All we have to do is just move one step towards it. Somebody said, "Move one step towards God; God will move ten steps towards you." And that is true for everything. Move one step towards your goal; your goal will move ten steps towards you.

> **King's Favorite Movie:**
> **The Lord of The Rings**

You always have the choice to feel better or to feel worse. Why in the world would we want to feel worse when we can feel happy? We have the power to make everything feel happy. When you're happy, you're in control of what you're doing. Have you ever tried to work on a thing when you're sad and depressed? It never works out. The ideas never come. So I never, ever take action when I am feeling bad. But you can do any bloody thing in the world when you're happy. It's like saying, "Bring it on. Anything in the world, you can throw at me!"

There's no reason in this world to live a life less than what you want to live. There's no reason for you to be less than what you want to be. Nobody can come into your head and make you less than that. It's only you who can think thoughts and only you who can take action. When you know that there is no outer factor affecting your life, then you know all is well. All you have to do is come to a new idea and move towards it.

CREATEENS

There's always going to be an unfulfilled idea that you are moving towards. This is endless. Some people believe that there is a checklist in life and when you are done you are gone from here. There's no checklist. Keep a carrot in front of a donkey and it never ends. It's not about the carrot, it's about moving in the direction of the carrot. It's not about the business you're pursuing, it's about the climb. It's about enjoying the process of becoming. You've always wanted to pursue your passion? You're doing it! Be happy for God's sake!

Being happy takes so-called "hard work" out off the equation. There is no hard work. You're thinking, "I'm going to work day and night and then I'm going to be successful." Fat chance. But if you think, "I love doing this. I love writing blog posts and I can forget to sleep when I'm doing that." Then it's automatic. It's labor of love. Ask Bill Gates: was building Windows hard work?

Q: Why do you call yourself an outlaw in India?
A: I consider myself an outlaw because I refuse to follow a given pattern. I'm going to reinvent the wheel. My vision of the wheel is unique.

The majority of India thinks, "I'm here. I better play this safe because this is the only life I've got. I better get in the rat race that everyone has tried and tested." How many students in your own class are really interested in enterprising? Or are 90% of them just there for the degree? They want to get a good job so that they can get a good life, good money, and be happy. I ask them, "Why don't you be happy in the first place?" Then you don't need the degree and you don't need the job. You can be happy now and you can do anything you want.

That's the reason I started *FRiEnDz* in the first place. I saw talented people wasting their time with work and trying to score marks in exams when they could do so much more. The magazine is a place where teenagers can be themselves. I want to make it a platform for teenagers to know that there is nothing better than following their own passion.

You're not going to find the real entrepreneurs in universities or online courses. Either you will find them as drop-outs or you will find them in the places least expected. Come to India. Go to the streets. They are street-smart people. They know how to sell. They can sell you your own shoes in two minutes.

Q: Where does the name King Sidharth come from?

A: It's self-imposed. Nobody named me King Sidharth. My name is Sidharth, the name of Buddha. It's my legal name, which I use everywhere. The physical personality – that you can talk to, see, and touch – is Sidharth. The personality that I know as myself, but that you cannot see, is King Sidharth.

King Sidharth is the non-physical entity where I come from, the ageless person. King Sidharth is someone who is eternal, who is timeless, and who is the summation of all of the lifetimes that I have ever lived. The best of things come from King Sidharth. Sidharth is just a medium to unfold that.

The name is a reminder to me about my real purpose in life. A king can do anything when he wants. It's not that I'm going to rule everyone else. It's that I'm going to rule myself. Nobody else is going to rule me but myself. That's what the 'King' means. You can call me Sid. My friends call me Sid.

Q: Anything else you would like to add?

A: When you start out, realize that you don't have to figure out everything in the first place. You can't. You can't sit at a breakfast table one morning and write out your life plan.

As you move on with your life, it will keep on changing. Creation is never complete. Keep on fine-tuning. If you're a designer, you will realize that design is never complete. If you are writing a blog post, you will realize that a blog post is never perfect. Google is the best company in the world. But, it is still evolving and it always will be evolving. So, you don't have to figure out all of the answers before you get started. All you have to figure out to begin with is what you want to do and then get started with it. The rest will come.

> **King's Favorite Website:**
> **Google**

If this universe inspired an idea in you, then it has every means to fulfill it. Trust in that. The more you improve, the faster you grow. So, the secret to business isn't finding the perfect plan and sticking to it. If you do that, your business is going to be dead. The secret is to keep on changing, keep on fine-tuning. The best scooter in India was Bajaj LML. For years, that was the only scooter you could get. But they didn't do any research and they didn't fine-tune their product. Every other company in India was doing just that. Today, LML has vanished from the market.

Entrepreneurship is never about playing it safe. If you want to play it safe, please close this book and go to sleep. It's not for you. Life is not for you. Life is never about playing it safe. Life is about playing it fun. That's behind every entrepreneur. If you go and ask, "What makes you so passionate about your blog, your product, or your business?" It's because they love changing it and they love how it all comes to form.

Be yourself, nothing else will do.

Website: KingSidharth.com, Createens.com
Twitter: @kingsidharth

KING SIDHARTH

*"The best way to predict the future
is to create it."*

- Peter Drucker

10

Teen Knocking on Google's Door
Arjun Rai, odysseyAds
West Windsor, New Jersey

BACKGROUND

Arjun Rai caught the entrepreneurial bug at the age of seven, selling knickknacks that he found around the house. Once, in his native India, young Arjun set up shop to sell leftover wildflower necklaces after a wedding. He and a cousin put up a banner at his grandmother's front gate, asking 25 cents.

TV shows like *The Oprah Show* and *The Big Idea with Donny Deutsch* inspired Arjun to take entrepreneurship to the next level. During the summer of 2009, he got a LinkedIn account (under the name Aaron Ray) and started connecting with other ambitious entrepreneurs, hoping to learn as much as possible about the art of entrepreneurship and business.

In 2010, Arjun became the COO of a quickly growing online advertising company, but he soon set out to follow his own, unique vision. That vision is a brand-new venture called odysseyAds. Though he's just getting started, Arjun plans to build odysseyAds into a premier online advertising network with a focus on customer service, maximizing ROI, and catering to 21st century marketer needs. In the midst of all this, Arjun also just completed his junior year of high school. He's 18 years old.

INTERVIEW

Q: What would you be doing right now if we weren't talking?

A: I go to West Windsor High School North and I just finished 11th grade. It was pretty hectic. So right now, I would either be doing something related to school or moving odysseyAds forward. I would be giving up the hours in the day, depending on my priorities – seeing which events or decisions would maximize my success.

Q: What drove you above and beyond, to entrepreneurship?

A: Some people put their dreams aside. They never find happiness. They never find the satisfaction that would come from starting their own company and doing something that they know is an extension of themselves. Going to high school, college, and then working nine-to-five is the career path for many, many people. But they're working for someone else, someone who could care less about their dreams and ideas.

There is a small group of people who try to build something with their passion, determination, and vision. For me, being ambitious means taking a risk and following a passion of mine. In most cases, that means building a company that caters to a need and is an extension of myself. It's going out there and taking a risk – regardless of any discouragement or negative opinion.

I started with computers at age seven. I moved on to learning more ad-

> *Arjun's Favorite Movie:*
> **The Pursuit of Happyness**

vanced topics in computer science. From a very young age, I would sell a few household items to the public. Sometimes I would get in trouble for that. There was one instance where I was in Denver, CO and we were moving. We had some items placed outside the front door that we were throwing out or that had to be packed. There was a pretty busy road right next to our apartment, so I put up a sign that advertised a few items for as little as 25 cents. A few people actually came up to the apartment. My dad and mom said, "Who are these people?" We had to turn them away.

Moving forward from there, I would watch *The Big Idea with Donny Deutsch*. It was a show on CNBC where entre-

ODYSSEYADS

preneurs came to share their business insights, promote entrepreneurship, and share their story of how they achieved the American Dream. These were young, brilliant people doing phenomenal things. So, Donny Deustch was a huge inspiration to me personally, through his books and through his show. From there, I got on LinkedIn and started meeting other entrepreneurs. Some were three times my age and others were only a few years older or younger than me. My horizons expanded gradually as I networked and gathered as much as possible about business and entrepreneurship.

Q: How do you balance your business with other priorities?

A: My business has definitely taken a toll on my grades. However, the journey has allowed me to become more aware of the world outside my room, my school, and my community. I have started to see that every decision I make has a "value proposition." Essentially, that means aligning tasks on a scale of importance and long-term benefit. I prioritize my tasks (homework, meeting people, etc.) so that the most important and beneficial always takes precedence over the others.

Q: What challenges have you faced specifically because of your age? How has your age helped you to succeed?

A: I found that starting young helped me meet new entrepreneurs and get their advice. Seldom do successful people turn aspiring entrepreneurs away due to their age. In fact, they're more receptive to giving their expert advice and sharing their stories. So, age has always been a major plus for me. Just don't stress that point too much or try to use it as an excuse for not meeting the client's needs.

Q: How have people around you reacted to your success?

A: Out of privacy concerns, I haven't told too many people around me that I'm involved in something as grand as this. The close friends that I've told have been very supportive You always want to surround yourself with people who are rooting for you and who want you to succeed. Stay away

ARJUN RAI

from the naysayers who couldn't do it themselves.

I am very lucky to have parents who are always there to support me and guide me along the way. My mom, Aparna, has always been a pillar of strength. I respect and love her very much for that. She supports me through thick and thin, giving me mentorship and advice on how to get through life both as an experienced adult and as a businesswoman herself. She has been helping me with the startup as well. There's a lot to learn from her because she is also an entrepreneur.

Surround yourself with family and friends who are there for you at any point, at any cost. Listen to those who are rooting for you and who aren't always criticizing you or trying to bring you down. It's important to stay close to your roots. There are too many examples in society of people letting money and success get to their head. They start giving out negative vibes to the people around them and that attracts negative events and circumstances

Arjun's Favorite Website: Forbes.com

So, it's very important to stay humble and grounded at the same time. Richard Branson, Bill Gates, Oprah Winfrey, Howard Schultz, Ryan Blair, Robert Herjavec, Barbara Corcoran, Gurbaksh Chahal, Daymond Johns, Will.i.am, Jay-Z, and others are examples of entrepreneurs who don't have to work another day in their life, but who are still passionate and humble.

Q: How did you plan and organize your business?
A: I think the most crucial thing is to have email, internet access, a cell phone, and other devices that enable you to communicate with people around the world. I highly recommend Gmail.

Having talked to so many entrepreneurs, it's fairly evident

that our world is getting smaller and smaller. In many instances, I find myself talking to someone who knows someone I have spoken to or will be speaking to in the future. So communication and networking are a must in this evolving world.

Q: What is the single most important reason for your success?

A: You have to know what you're trying to build and why you're trying to build it. The most important components in my entrepreneurial endeavors have been my passion and a drive to make it big. I was very ambitious from a very young age. I have a lot of dreams and ideas and the only way I can accomplish them is to have passion and love for my work. There is no point in doing something you don't love or care about; then, you are doing it solely for the money.

> *Arjun's Favorite TV Show:*
> **Shark Tank**

Success never comes to you for free. You need hard work and hard work is so much easier when you're passionate about your work. Otherwise, when you mix in greed and negative energy, you're setting yourself up for failure. You should love every moment of your "work" and share that fun with others as well.

Q: What would you tell an up-and-coming entrepreneur?

A: Just put yourself out there. It doesn't matter what age you are. Reach out to people who have been there and done it. There is no point in hiding your ideas or being afraid. It's the execution of the idea that separates one individual from another. If you are trying to start a business, start a business that you are passionate about. Hard work is a product of passion. Finally, make sure your business idea is viable within an industry that is big. Seldom do new inventions or ideas that create an entirely new industry work out. Take an existing idea and do it better than anyone else, with unwavering passion and drive.

ARJUN RAI

Growing up, I was always talking to people and reaching out to people for their advice. Without that experience and expertise, it would have been very, very difficult to build a business that would succeed. Knowledge is power – so long as it doesn't prohibit you from actually going out there and taking the risk. Don't be afraid to network with other people who are in the same industry or who have a similar passion. Gaining advice and gaining mentorship is critical – especially for young entrepreneurs.

Q: If you had to battle a giant, what weapon would you use?

A: I would use my mind. In any situation, whether it's meeting a new person or taking a company to the next level, it's you and your way of thinking that will differentiate you from others. Similarly, your way of thinking, or the mind, will give rise to creative ways of "fighting" the giant. Adapting to the environment or utilizing a tool to fight the giant all comes to the individual through practical, logical, and creative thinking. And for that, the mind is crucial.

Q: What do you want to be when you grow up?

A: I have already set my career path as an entrepreneur. It's a career where people work their entire life and never get tired of it. The entrepreneur always puts an extension of himself or herself into any business that he or she starts. So for me, my entire life will be comprised of amazing endeavors that I will be involved with because I love the ideas and feel passionate about them.

Q: What would you say to someone who's thinking about quitting their job and starting an entrepreneurial venture?

A: Don't go out there for greed. If you're trying to build a company or if you're quitting a job, follow your passion. It really comes down to taking a risk and having the support of your friends and your family. But, all in all, it's a decision for yourself that you have to make. It's definitely a risky move, so you have to measure your risks and not do something completely stupid.

With entrepreneurship, you get a reward for how much you put in. It's not like a conventional career, where you don't necessarily see the rewards of your hard work. There's a high potential that you will get back that hard work with entrepreneurship – so long as you're passionate about it and not just looking for where the next dollar is coming from.

Q: You're starting a new company right now? What's that like?
A: I'm looking forward to building odysseyAds and launching it as soon as possible. The founding goal is to gain the clients' satisfaction and really cater to the needs of the 21st century marketer, maximizing their return on investment. We want to provide a service that clients find useful to their marketing efforts. Whether you are a publisher (website owner) or an advertiser, we intend to create a service that brings efficiency to the process and assists the client in their needs. Like any startup, there's a lot of uncertainty behind it, but there's a lot of passion behind it at the same time.

> *Arjun's Favorite Book:*
> **The Dream**
> *by Gurbaksh Chahal*

I always think positively in any situation, because that's all you can do – all you should do. So, I'm thinking very positively about this new venture and I look forward to scaling it as far as I can. For anyone starting out: it doesn't matter if you're 18, 12, or 50, and it doesn't matter where you are, who you are, or what idea you have. What matters is that you have passion for it and you aren't doing it for greed. If you have a bad month in sales, you need to have enough passion to keep moving forward. When you combine passion with hard work, it's so much easier to run something at a larger scale.

ARJUN RAI

Q: Anything else you would like to add?

A: To any aspiring entrepreneur, you need to have passion and a drive to make it big. Go out there with so much passion that nobody can stop you. Don't be afraid to reach out to other people – whether they're billionaires, millionaires, or aspiring entrepreneurs themselves. They can give you advice and mentorship. As you move forward with your business and your life, look at the "value proposition" when making decisions. Have a plan A, B, and C so that you are never in a state of confusion when something doesn't go as antici- pated. Whether in life or business, plan everything!

Don't let yourself worry about people who are trying to bring you down. At the end of the day, it's your life – your story that you have to write, your song that you have to sing, and your dance that you have to dance. Make your business for yourself. You will find a lot of people who will try to bring you down because they can't do it themselves. Ignore them and move on. Even if you fail, at least you tried. So many other people didn't take that chance, put themselves out there, and follow their dreams with passion. Always learn from your mistakes and get up the next day. Implement those les- sons to attain success and make it big. Good luck!

Website: odysseyAds.com
Twitter: @arjunrai96

"This interview really does embody what the future of business is going to look like: marketing that is centered around the customer of small-to-medium proportions instead of focusing on all of the big players. I admire his enthusiasm for the details, while at the same time never losing site of a BIG picture and striving to make it bigger for everyone."

**~ Brandon W,
Comment on JuniorBiz**

ODYSSEYADS

11

Social Media Prodigy & WordPress Wizard
Syed Balkhi, Uzzz Productions
Palm Beach, Florida

BACKGROUND

Syed Balkhi used to get online at three o'clock in the morning to trade stones for a game called Neopets. When he was 12, his cousin pointed out that he could do the same thing with domain names – all while pulling in a handsome profit. Soon he was developing websites, designing them, and running a paid domain name directory.

Originally from Pakistan, Syed is now 19 and attending the University of Florida in Gainesville. Along with a handful of college friends (Amanda Roberts, David Pegg, and Mohammed Karim), Syed has started a successful web service company called Uzzz Productions. His blog about WordPress, WPBeginner, has been up since July 2009 and already attracts an incredible 145,000 unique visitors each month. Maybe it's genetic: Syed's six-year-old brother is running a successful blog of his own, with Syed's help.

INTERVIEW

Q: What would you be doing right now if we weren't talking?

A: Actually, I would be coding a website for my college's psychology department.

Q: What drove you above and beyond, to entrepreneurship?

A: My allowance was pretty low. I wasn't a big gamer-type person. I was more of an eater-type person. I was so addicted to Mountain Dew and I wanted more Mountain Dew than my allowance money allowed. So [entrepreneurship] was just another way for me to get money. Imagine you're a kid. $500 or $1000 a month is really big when you're 13 years old. So that was my biggest motivation.

NeoPets was the foundation, actually. I was designing my own [NeoPets-themed] wallpaper, just for myself. Then I got into the design industry. My experience in all of these different industries has allowed me to really converse with my developers from a developers standpoint, with my marketers from a marketers standpoint, and so on.

Q: How do you balance your business with other priorities?

A: In the beginning it was really, really hard. In high school, you have to be in school from 7:00 am until 2:00 pm. That is the time when a lot of online business is taking place. I didn't have a laptop, because back in those days laptops were really expensive. So, I used to work on the computers in the library before school and during lunch time. That's one of the ways I was balanced.

> **Syed's Favorite Book:**
> **The Alchemist**
> *by Paulo Coehlo*

But for school homework, I really didn't do a lot of it. I managed to get a 3.98 GPA when I graduated. But when there was a school project coming up and I also had a design project for another client, my business was definitely affecting my schoolwork. I would just go over the money: my high school teacher was not paying me. Even now, I think that my business is affecting my studies significantly because I have to travel a lot, so I'm missing classes. But I also think that it is affecting my studies in a positive way. It's not just theory. I can apply my practical life experience to the theoretical parts and do pretty well in classes.

Q: What challenges have you faced specifically because of your age? How has your age helped you to succeed?

UZZZ PRODUCTIONS

A: One of the big challenges that I faced was that I wasn't considered seriously in the industry. I bet that if I was 34 years
old, people would have taken me seriously. I was running
sites that were bigger than the ones most of these 40-year-
old guys were running. But because of my young age and
my language barrier (my grammar wasn't very good) people
would think, "Oh, this is just some 14-year-old kid." Another
disadvantage that it has caused me is that I couldn't attend
a lot of conferences. I'm an affiliate marketer but I haven't
gone to any affiliate summits because you have to be 21.

The best thing about my age is that I don't have a lot of responsibilities. I don't have a kid to pay for; I don't have my
bills. When I was 12 years old, I was living under my parents'
roof. I wasn't paying for my internet bill, my apartment bill,
or much of anything.

A lot of people have said that the internet is a teenager.
Guess who understands a teenager best: a teenager. I was
seeing things from a different view that a lot of older people
were not able to see. I would see what was becoming the
next cool thing and I would focus on it.

Q: **How have people around you reacted to your success?**
A: My parents are definitely very happy. Sometimes they don't
understand what exactly I'm doing, but they're happy that
I'm doing it. The local newspaper did an entire front page
article on me, which was pretty cool. Then, I got invited by
numerous high schools to come give a speech to all of the
young students there and help them out.

I bought a brand-new Honda Civic when I was 16 years old.
I bought it in cash. People asked me, "Dude, what are your
payments on that?" I said, "I don't have any payments." That
created a lot of buzz.

The negative reaction comes from people trying to exclude

you, in a way. If you are getting that much publicity, you're friends might think that you were like a level above them even if you don't think so. That is the disappointing part about it.

Q: How did you plan and organize your business?

A: I go with the flow. When I was a kid, I thought that organizational tactics were just a lot of BS from older folks saying, "You're supposed to this and that." So in the beginning, I would just get a domain name and start putting a design on it. I wouldn't have any business plan; I wouldn't know how to monetize it. That was the reason why a lot of my time was wasted. Some of those projects weren't even worth all of the time I was spending on them.

I'm still probably not the most organized person in this world, but now I keep track of what I'm doing and I have a list of things. Ideas used to come to me and then go away. So I started carrying a notepad and that notepad is getting filled so fast. Having plans definitely gets everything done faster. If you don't have a planner, get a planner. If you don't like using a planner, just get a sheet of paper and start writing.

Since I started being more organized, all of my projects are going really well. I registered WPBeginner in early 2009. I got the business plan, wrote the entire idea, how I was going to make money off of it, the purpose of the site, and my six month goal. Once you get to that six month mark, then you want to re-evaluate whether you have met your goals and what to do next.

In terms of online tools, Google Docs is really, really cool. I also use Excel a lot.

Q: What is the single most important reason for your success?

A: Social media. If it wasn't for Twitter, LinkedIn, and Facebook, I wouldn't have been able to get in touch with a lot of these

UZZZ PRODUCTIONS

top guys who I now have the pleasure to know and talk to. Social media deserves a lot of credit because it opened all of the doors for me. If you notice, a lot of young artists have made it big by being on YouTube and getting publicity. This is free advertising. Absolutely free. A lot of people don't notice it.

Q: What would you tell an up-and-coming entrepreneur?
A: Don't get arrogant. That's one of the mistakes that I made in my early years. When you're young and you're making a lot of money, you might get that feeling that you know it all. The reality is that you don't. You should always stay hungry. Stay hungry, so you can eat. Wherever you go, you can learn so much from the people who you would expect the least from. But the only way you will learn is if you go in with the mindset that you're going to learn.

> *Syed's Favorite Food:*
> *French Fries*

SYED BALKHI

Also, you need to make sure that you understand what you're doing before you do it. I learned a lot of things from my mistakes, but I wish that I hadn't tried to reinvent the wheel. It's more efficient to spend more time learning from other people's mistakes and then go from there. So now I talk to other people and ask what mistakes they have made.

Q: If you had to battle a giant, what weapon would you use?
A: I'm a giant myself. I'm 6'4", so I don't know. I don't think I would need a weapon. My mind is the biggest weapon that I have. I am a firm believer in the self. Your self is a reflection of your mind and your creativity. So, it's not about what weapon you have; it's about how you use it. I could probably use a paper and give you a paper cut, but if I didn't know how to pull a trigger then a gun would be useless to me.

The only way I know how to produce results is by doing it my way. A lot of people try to make the mistake of trying to follow somebody. But a lot of these techniques simply can't be replicated. So doing what you do best is the best way for you to succeed. Improvisation and creativity will take you beyond anything else.

Q: What do you want to be when you grow up?

A: That's a tough question. I don't want to grow up. I like the way I am. I want to be an entrepreneur and I don't want to work for anybody else. I love that I can work from wherever I want, whenever I want. I'm making money when I'm sleeping. It's a great feeling when you can wake up and say, "Oh wow – I just made $600 while I was sleeping. I was a productive sleeper!"

> *Syed's Favorite Website:*
> *Google*

Entrepreneurship has really opened a lot of doors for me. To give you a personal example, I got a traffic citation. I knew a lawyer who was my client. So, I didn't have to find a lawyer to fight my ticket. Same with my finance guy and my insurance guy. I get the best discounts you can get on my travelling, on my car insurance – on everything. If I was working as an employee, I would not even know how my boss was making money. Now I see a bigger picture.

Another thing is that I get a lot of technology before everyone else because all of these companies get it as a gift for me. Mountain Dew sent me a Flip camera and eight never before tasted Mountain Dew flavors. I helped decide which flavor should be on the shelf. That was a great opportunity and I owe it to entrepreneurship and social media. I was really happy. I love Mountain Dew.

Q: What would you tell a young entrepreneur who is just getting started with social media?

A: Use social media as a communication tool rather than a marketing tool. When you are using Twitter, don't set autotweets every time you publish a blog post. If you had a customer on a call, you wouldn't tell him, "Hey – I don't have time for you. Bye." That's how I see social media: if I have 4,500 followers, that's like 4,000 clients for me. I don't want to treat them with disrespect. So, I actually spend the 30 seconds that it takes me to write a clean title, show them my URL, and tweet that.

Second, a lot of people try to get on Digg's front page. But Digg can do nothing for your Search Engine Optimization (SEO). Stop submitting your own articles, because that's not the way to go. It's meant to be shared. No matter how good of an author you are, not all of your articles deserve to be on Digg. Keep your promotion for only the best articles. You're building a brand – and when you have a brand, people just talk about you. That is what you really want.

Don't go after the quantity, go after the quality. People are following 120,000 people to get 120,001 followers. But because you don't have a real connection with those 120,001 people, it's not going to do you any good. I would rather have 200 converted followers who, when I send them a message, they go and do it.

Q: How have you built professional relationships with some of the biggest names on the internet?

A: You have to think about what you are offering them first. Why should they even write about your product? You could just ask for a link exchange and you might get it, but not once you get to bigger sites. So, you have to offer something in return.

I was talking to Robert Scoble after his site had been hacked. Just out of courtesy, I said, "Hey Robert, I saw your site got hacked and I know a few things about internet security. This is what I would do to prevent it." I didn't expect anything back from Robert Scoble. But he went on Twitter and said, "Hey – check out WPBeginner." That was huge.

SYED BALKHI

83

Q: Your six-year-old brother Zain is blogging. Why get started with entrepreneurship early?

A: I got him started at four. He was in preschool and he could read, but he could not write at all. So we would make video blogs of him — just silly videos. Now he has his own laptop which he can use and he's getting all of these presents from companies. So, I think he sees that entrepreneurship is something that is worthwhile.

I learn from him, too. My site is all about beginners and I think that I passed that level a while back [laughs]. So it's harder for me to understand a lot of these things from a beginner's perspective. There are some design issues that he has pointed out. It's a learning experience from a six-year-old.

When you're starting someone as an athlete, you're going to start them as young as you can. The younger they are the better, because they are able to pick it up a lot faster. But I am not pushing my brother to go into entrepreneurship. I also got him a basketball court in the backyard, along with hockey and soccer equipment. I am showing him all of the routes and I'm going to help him whichever way he chooses to go.

Q: Anything else you would like to add?

A: I think we talked about pretty much everything. I want to give a shout-out to WPBeginner. If anyone is starting to blog and wants to learn the technical aspects, I don't think they should go pay someone $400 to take a mini-course. Everything that you need is free on the site, so go check it out. We also set up WordPress blogs for anyone who signs up for one of our hosting services. You would be paying for the hosting services anyway, so you might as well go through us and we'll set up the site for you.

Website: WPBeginner.com, Uzzz.net
Twitter: @syedbalkhi

"Awesome interview Nick! This dude had so much good knowledge to share. He seems like a social media genius. He is so right about Twitter and your followers. I figured that out the hard way."

~ Alex,
Comment on JuniorBiz

SYED BALKHI

*"Opportunity is missed by most people
because it is dressed in overalls
and looks like work."*

- Thomas Edison

12

Entrepreneur of all Trades
Keith J. Davis Jr., K. Jerrold Enterprises Inc.
Houston, Texas

BACKGROUND
Keith J. Davis Jr. grew up watching his father sell watches, clothing, and anything else he could get his hands on. Following in his dad's footsteps, ten-year-old Keith ventured to a wholesale market, where he bought a dozen hats at a few bucks a pop. He sold them all back for about $10 in profit each. Instead of being satisfied with his success, Keith kept selling: at school, he sold everything from Yu-Gi-Oh cards to magnetic earrings to bubble gum.

Today, Keith is 19 and he's gone from his middle school's "bubble gum man" to a college freshman at the University of Houston and an entrepreneur of all trades. He somehow finds time to be a nationally known public speaker, actor, model, newspaper publisher, and author. His newspaper, *Fyt Ya* (renaming to *Idealist Magazine*), and his book, *Young? So What!*, are both aimed towards empowering young people to become successful entrepreneurs.

INTERVIEW
Q: What would you be doing right now if we weren't talking?
A: I would be developing and redesigning *Fyt Ya*. My business partner, Josue Alvarado, and I are trying to get the publication back up and running. We have been coming together and doing a lot of research about newspapers in decline. We know that there is still a need out there. Teen literacy has been declining. Teen media, especially when it comes to

KEITH J. DAVIS JR.

news and print, has been declining. We're trying to fill that void when it comes to entrepreneurship and business. We're trying to really have an impact on this generation with our publication.

Q: What drove you above and beyond, to entrepreneurship?

A: I started off at a young age. I found my niche and I fell in love with entrepreneurship. My driving force is creating another generation of entrepreneurs. I believe this generation's exposure to new technology and the advancement of business is great. So I just want to continue to push [that forward].

My father owns a large marketing communication firm called D-Mars. He didn't start off as an

> *Keith's Favorite TV Show:*
> **Family Guy**

entrepreneur, but he has always had the entrepreneurial spirit. My mom was a late bloomer, but now she's a real estate consultant. All of us had go-getter spirit. There's a lot of love and a lot of ambition [in our family]. Coming from an urban community and not having much growing up, my parents always wanted something different – not just for themselves, but for me and for future generations. That spirit was passed on to me.

Q: How do you balance your business with other priorities?

A: I get this question a lot from students. You have to prioritize and evaluate what's important in your life at that time. A lot of young folks get caught up in the hype of entertainment and the night life. I always tell people that the night life isn't going anywhere. As long as people are on this planet, we're going to party and we're going to have fun. But you have to have balance. You have to have structure.

School and education are crucial. My business is crucial. But you also have to be able to live your life and enjoy it. I've always felt like my vision was in line with my education and

K. JERROLD ENTERPRISES, INC.

my community relationships. There were conflicts. I didn't attend a lot of events or activities during my junior and senior years of high school. But that was my decision. I thought that taking care of some other things was more important. I'm definitely trying to take advantage of [school activities] more while I'm in college. I am getting involved with different organizations and continuing to prioritize to the best of my ability.

Q: What challenges have you faced specifically because of your age? How has your age helped you to succeed?

A: Being young is a challenge in and of itself. Especially at 15 or 16, you're going to be going through some of those awkward phases. Sometimes being young, being ambitious, and trying to do everything can hurt you.

I remember at one point I was trying to do too much and spreading myself too thin. I was thinking about getting involved in real estate, trying to re-establish *Fyt Ya*, promoting my book, speaking, and going to school. All of that was just too much. As young people, that's what we do: we think that we're all superheroes and we can do everything. But you've still got to have structure and focus.

My father taught me at a young age that it's not about what you know, but who you know. I get a lot of support because of my age. Especially as a young African American, people see that I'm trying to do something positive and help a generation. So professionals are willing to lend a hand and lend their advice. If I was 20 or 30 years old, they would be charging me for that advice.

> *Keith's Favorite Book:*
> **Young? So What!**
> *by Keith J. Davis Jr.*

Q: How have people around you reacted to your success?

A: I've been truly blessed with good people around me. My

89

friends, peers, and family continue to support what I'm doing. A lot of students [at my high school] didn't know what I did, because I wasn't the type to broadcast what I was doing. When people did find out and said, "Oh that's Keith on TV," I would get some funny faces. You always try to stay down-to-earth and humble because, God willing, it could all be taken away any day. So I try to keep a level head.

I guess my greatest accomplishment is that February 19th was declared Keith J. Davis Jr. Day in Houston. It felt good to know that some of the things I was doing through the publication and through my community involvement were getting recognized. I got a proclamation. I keep it at the office. There are only 365 days a year and I got one of them, so it felt pretty good.

Q: How did you plan and organize your business?
A: You've got to be up-to-date with technology. There are so many tools out there to help grow a business that you can't afford to be stuck in the dinosaur age – especially our generation. [You need to] find out what's new and what's going on. You have to know what's creative and what's really going to attract this generation. You've got to be up-to-date on social media. You just have to roll with the tide and try to keep up.

We study a lot of different publications. I wasn't always a big fan of reading, to be honest. But I do it because it educates me. It helps me stay informed. I'm also constantly meeting with other entrepreneurs to figure out what's next, what's new. I'm always trying to collaborate with people and brainstorm great ideas.

Q: What is the single most important reason for your success?
A: Ambition. I'm super-ambitious. I've had it in my mind from a young age that there's nothing out there that I couldn't have if I worked hard enough to get it. So I have big goals, dreams, and aspirations in life. We live in a generation where there

K. JERROLD ENTERPRISES, INC.

are individuals worth billions and they are able to make an immensely positive change in the world. Nothing could ever tell me that I can't do that as well. I'm trying to make a difference and leave a legacy.

Q: What would you tell an up-and-coming entrepreneur?

A: If you have a goal, be relentless in your pursuit. You've just got to go at it hard. Don't let anybody say that you can't. There's opportunity there. There will be obstacles that are going to hinder you, but we're all given resources to overcome those things.

> **Keith's Favorite Band: Kings of Leon**

Distractions. Whether it is worldly obsessions, peer pressure, or their environment, a lot of young adults are being distracted from their goals and their visions. They have what I call a 'light bulb idea', where something great or extraordinary crosses their minds. The problem is that few of them bring it into existence because of distractions or because they're resting on their talents.

Q: If you had to battle a giant, what weapon would you use?

A: Maybe my Mac, because it does everything. Maybe it would be a great defense too [laughs]. I would also try to use my communication skills and maybe I could charm it with my smile. Communicating effectively is one of the most important factors in being an entrepreneur and in being an individual. If you can't communicate, you're going to find yourself a lonely businessperson.

Q: What do you want to be when you grow up?

A: I want to be a philanthropist. When people talk about Keith J. Davis Jr., I want them to say that he was a great businessman, but that he also did a lot for the community and for his generation. I want to be able to make a difference by informing, encouraging, and inspiring others. I definitely want to leave a legacy.

KEITH J. DAVIS JR.

At some point I'm going to be working to get my real estate license. You build wealth through property, real estate, investments, and things of that nature. So, I want to get into commercial real estate. We own a marketing research firm. I can continue to learn the business and, one day, take it over.

Q: You are remarkably polite. Why? How has it helped you?

A: Being in the public eye, you've got to be cautious about some of the things you say and do. I'm always trying to be aware of my surroundings. I am also just being a genuinely kind person. My mom always said that you should treat people in the way you want to be treated, with respect.

Politeness has a long-term effect. Your first impression is an important one. I've come to find that you never know who someone is or who someone knows, so you want to be respectful to everyone. You never know how you might need that person or how that person might come into play in your life. For all I know, they could be Bill Gates' third cousin.

Q: What does the entrepreneurial mindset mean to you?

A: I've definitely learned the effects of a positive mindset. It's so crucial to me that it's the first chapter of *Young? So What!*. In business, things are not always going to go the way you planned it. You've always got to keep a level head and a positive outlook on things. As young people, we get frustrated easily and we're ready to throw in the towel. But having a positive attitude has brought me success. I know that no matter what the conflict, there is a way to resolve it.

> *Keith's Favorite Website:*
> *BlackVoices.com*

Q: Anything else you would like to add?

A: You know what they say: if you love what you do, you'll never work a day in your life. I'm in love with entrepreneurship and everything that comes with it. Entrepreneurship is where it's at right now, especially with this economy. The unemployment rate is at 10%. As students, we can't depend on finding a job right out of college. So, you've got to be able to create opportunities where there are none. There is definitely going to be an increase in individuals owning and operating their own businesses. Entrepreneurship is the key.

Any time young people are doing something positive and spreading the word of entrepreneurship in our generation, I feel like it's my duty to help out. I'm just honored to be able to be a part of this program.

Website: keithjdavisjr.com, fytya.com
Twitter: @keithjdavisjr

> *"It's definitely cool to see how many people started out young selling things like gaming cards, console items, and so on (for me, it was Pokémon cards). Keith definitely seems talented and I'm sure we'll be hearing a lot more about him (and a few others featured on this site) over the next few years."*
>
> **~ Jason P,**
> **Comment on JuniorBiz**

KEITH J. DAVIS JR.

93

*"I'm not a businessman.
I'm a business, man."*

- Jay-Z

13

Major League Young Entrepreneur
Ben Weissenstein, Grand Slam Garage Sales
Houston, Texas

BACKGROUND
Every kid has started a lemonade stand. Usually it isn't front page news. But at the age of four, Ben Weissenstein was featured on the cover of *The Houston Chronicle*, touting lemonade for 25 cents a cup. Ben only earned a few dollars, but he came away with a thirst for entrepreneurship that motivates him to this day.

When Ben was 14, he helped his mom with a garage sale. She suggested that he could help friends and neighbors sell and organize their extra junk. So Ben and his friend started a business. In a few years, Grand Slam Garage Sales had expanded to offer more services and employ over 30 part-time workers.

Now 19, Ben and his booming business have been featured in *Entrepreneur Magazine* and on *Dr. Phil*. He has started The Entitled Group, a company that helps musical artists like Mike Jones, Lil' Flip, and Young Hash book concerts and other events. Ben has moved from Houston, TX to Tucson, AZ, where he is helping launch the first of many Grand Slam Garage Sales franchises.

INTERVIEW
Q: What would you be doing right now if we weren't talking?
A: I would be on the phone and replying to emails at the same time. That's basically what I do all day: calling people, following up with people, reading emails, and trying to make things

happen. The Blackberry is the perfect tool.

Q: What drove you above and beyond, to entrepreneurship?

A: I've never liked to work for anyone. I worked for a grocery store at one point, bagging groceries. But I felt like I could do a lot more if I just went after it on my own. My parents got divorced when I was 13 and that's when I got more motivated to do something big with my life. I've always believed in myself and my ability to build an empire. I ended up starting the garage sale business.

> **Ben's Favorite Book:**
> **Good to Great**
> **by Jim Collins**

I'm willing to do everything that it takes to succeed – as long as it's moral and legal. I feel like there's really no one who is as driven as me. I'm willing to stay up all night. I've learned that anything's possible if you put in the work and you think creatively. If one route doesn't work, you can just go another route.

For example, if we send a letter to the editor of *Fortune Magazine* and we don't get a response, we will just look up another contact at *Fortune Magazine* and contact them. If that doesn't work, we'll find another contact at the magazine until someone responds. Don't take no for an answer.

Q: How do you balance your business with other priorities?

A: Friends and family are the most important things. But it has always been hard for me to motivate myself for school. I've gotten pretty good grades, but I'm not a straight-A student. I was a sophomore this year at the University of Arizona in Tucson, but I decided to take the semester off because I was getting too busy. I will probably come back next year – but, as of now, I just want to get all of the businesses to a point where I can balance them better with school.

I've taken business classes and they've taught me things that

I hadn't learned [with my businesses]. But I could argue all day saying that I've learned much, much, more in real life than I ever have in school. I'm not denouncing school. I am just more driven to make money and build companies.

Q: **What challenges have you faced specifically because of your age? How has your age helped you to succeed?**

A: At one point, my mom had to sign all of the checks for Grand Slam Garage Sales because I wasn't 18. You have to be 18 to sign the checks on the bank account. That was a little hurdle.

There have also been certain instances where I haven't gotten as much respect as I would have gotten if I were older. But

> *Ben's Favorite Food:*
> *Chinese Food*

it's not happening as much anymore because I'm starting to gain more credibility, which helps to diminish the age factor. That's exactly why we market everything so professionally. We have a very nice website. The workers come in uniform. They talk very politely and have good manners.

Certain people have probably been more willing to give me advice because of my age. Brian Scudamore, the CEO of 1-800-GOT-JUNK?, has always lent advice to me. He's a really nice guy. To the press, my story wouldn't be as interesting if I wasn't 19. If I was a 40-year-old who started a garage sale company, I wouldn't be that cool.

Q: **How have people around you reacted to your success?**

A: My family and friends are definitely proud. There have also been random people who call me up for advice and say that I inspired them. That's the stuff that I love to hear.

I've also seen a sort of jealousy. For example, I had some kid come up to me and egg me on, saying, "Hey, Ben the CEO! I can get cheaper prices on rappers than you can." I just laughed. Stuff like that doesn't really bother me. If anything,

BEN WEISSENSTEIN

I get motivated by it.

Q: How did you plan and organize your business?

A: Everything started as nothing. Our principles were professionalism, keeping records, and keeping our customers and workers happy. We just figured it out as we went. When I started Grand Slam Garage Sales with my friend Matt, we went to Walmart and bought two red polo shirts for about eight dollars apiece [as uniforms]. We thought we looked professional, at least. The red polo shirts turned into blue uniforms with Grand Slam Garage Sales logos.

We knew we had to keep records to an extent, so we started by opening a Word document and writing, "We took in x amount of dollars, we had x amount of expenses." Eventually that turned into a nice Excel spreadsheet, which turned into software that we had developed so we could put in [financial] information.

> **Ben's Favorite TV Show:**
> **The Real World**

Our first website was all right, but it was nothing special. We had a friend do it. Then we had another web guy do it, who did a better job. Then we had another web guy do it who did an even better job. Basically, I started out not knowing much and I just kept learning as I went along. That's the biggest thing: always learn, change, and grow with your business.

Q: What is the single most important reason for your success?

A: My drive and determination. There have been so many times when I almost failed. When we first started, we were taking in money but we didn't know how to manage it. Nothing was organized. But something always told me to keep going and find a way to make it work. After that, [the next most important thing is] constant work. I've always been driven and I feel like that is going to be the key to major success.

Q: What would you tell an up-and-coming entrepreneur?

A: Always be honest. Have morals. If you do bad business, it will come back to bite you. There will be a lot of opportunities where you can make something work by doing something a little bit shady, but those things will end up hurting you and your company in the long run. You'll gain a lot of respect by being honest. Whatever business you have, you have to treat it like a real business. Don't take short cuts

You're not going to be successful right when you start. I don't care what anybody says. It's not like Mark Zuckerberg built Facebook in one night and it was what it is now. There's no such thing as an overnight success. Sometimes "overnight success" actually means a few years. But if you can come to terms with the fact that you've got to put in a lot of work to make something happen, then you can become a successful entrepreneur.

Q: If you had to battle a giant, what weapon would you use?

A: Being creative, there's always a way to make something happen. Maybe I would go to the gym first, before I fought the giant. I could go over to L.A. Fitness and do the bench press a few times. In all of my companies, the biggest thing is the drive and the creativity. For every problem, there's a solution. It's just about finding that solution.

Q: What do you want to be when you grow up?

A: I used to want to be a Major League Baseball player [laughs]. Now, I definitely want to be a CEO who owns multiple successful multi-millionaire dollar companies. One of my goals with Grand Slam Garage Sales is to sell 500 franchises across multiple countries. I want The Entitled Group to be one of the biggest event planning and artist management companies in the country. At the same time, I want to be a major philanthropist and help a lot of people. It sounds cheesy, but it's the truth.

BEN WEISSENSTEIN

My brother told me, "Live a life worth reading." To me, that means that I can't just build some businesses, buy some Ferraris, and die. It means that I want to make tons of money, own baseball teams, and help a lot of people at the same time. For instance, my grandma has a little company called 'Women on the Way Up' that helps women who are in poverty and girls in school. I want to help get that program across the country. I also want to create homeless shelters that have schools and rehabilitation services. That way, homeless people will not only have a place to sleep, but they will also be empowered to turn their lives around.

Q: You've employed a few of your friends. How do you maintain the balance between employee and friend?

A: A few of my close friends are going to be in charge of the Tucson Grand Slam Garage Sales location. I definitely prefer to work with friends in certain circumstances, but I'm not going to hire a random friend just because he's my friend. I'm looking for a friend who will do a good job and who has all of the necessary skills.

> *Ben's Favorite Website: Entrepreneur.com*

For the friends who I've worked with, I've always made the line between business and friendship very clear. For example, when I was in high school, I had a lot of friends working for me, running the garage sales. There were times when they would mess up at work. I would have to ask them, "Hey – why did you do this?" They didn't get treated differently than any other worker. But the second the garage sale was over, we would go out to Fuddruckers and eat burgers together. Once business is over, we're friends again.

Q: How did you get in *Entrepreneur Magazine* and on *Dr. Phil*?

A: A lot of the press we've gotten has been random press that has just come to us. It wasn't from us sending out a press release. For example, I was just at my high school reading an email that said, "We want to do a story on you and blah,

blah, blah." Then I saw *Entrepreneur Magazine* at the bottom. I was so excited that I told all of my friends. That definitely brought more credibility to the table and got the word out about Grand Slam Garage Sales.

Dr. Phil was completely random. I think they found out about us when they were searching the internet and saw the interviews we did on *FOX News* in Houston. They did a story on us that was a lot of fun and got us a lot more prospective franchisees.

But before we really start franchising here, we're going to be calling all sorts of press and getting our company's name out there. The more press we get, the more credibility we have. Good publicity is good. I don't believe that bad publicity is good.

Q: Anything else you would like to add?
A: Anyone can go check out my personal website and the official website of Ben the CEO Ventures, which is BenTheCEO.com. You can also check out EntitledGroup.com, GrandSlamGarageSales.com, and follow me at Twitter.com/bentheceo.

Website: BenTheCEO.com, GrandSlamGarageSales.com
Twitter: @bentheceo

"Another great interview Nick! It's surprising how we all get our entrepreneurial inspirations. I personally got a taste into business by first selling greeting cards when I was way younger!!"

~ Martin,
Comment on JuniorBiz

"Excellence is a habit."

- Aristotle

14

Fired at 13, Founder at 14
Sabirul Islam, The World at Your Feet
London, United Kingdom

BACKGROUND

Sabirul Islam grew up in a crime-ridden borough of London, England. His eyes were opened to entrepreneurship by his cousin, who offered Sabirul a job at the age of 13. But when Sabirul was fired a few weeks later, he decided to take matters into his own hands. At 14, he gathered six of his friends and started Veyron Technology, a website design company. Sabirul made his first $1,000 within the first two weeks.

In January of 2008, at age 17, Sabirul self-published his first book. *The World at Your Feet* offers young people guidance and encouragement to turn their entrepreneurial vision into reality. It's safe to say that Sabirul is an expert on the subject: not only has the book sold 60,000 copies, Sabirul has also launched a board game (*Teen-Trepreneur*), become a globe-trotting public speaker (over 600 speaking engagements), and started his own publishing company for aspiring teen authors.

Now 19, Sabirul keeps busy by developing an interactive web-site for young entrepreneurs, writing three additional books, and otherwise setting out to conquer the world.

INTERVIEW
Q: What would you be doing right now if we weren't talking?
A: I would probably be off at a speaking engagement trying to promote my four brands (*The World at Your Feet*, the board game *Teen-Trepreneur*, my online interactive site, and my-

self, Sabirul Islam). Each one has a separate vision to inspire, educate, and provide an opportunity. It's part of a process to nurture a young person from a virtual nobody into a somebody and to make them feel successful in life. I'm trying to expand the message to as many young people as possible around the world.

Q: What drove you above and beyond, to entrepreneurship?

A: When I was 13, I always looked up to my cousin, who was a year older than me. When he was 14, he had the audacity to start his first business. He was the managing director of his company and that blew me away. So, I just went up to him and said, "Cousin, can I work for you?" He gave me the job on the spot. I kind of took it for granted because he was my cousin and I thought that the money would just roll into my back pocket. Well, two weeks later he sent me an official letter through my post, with his company logo and signed by him. All it said was, "Dear Sabirul Islam, you're fired."

I was hired and fired at the age of 13 by my own flesh and blood. That was the toughest thing to take. It opened my eyes to entrepreneurship. I said, "I don't ever want to work for somebody else for the rest of my life." You can get bossed around by them and you just have to do what they say.

> *Sabirul's Favorite Food: Italian Food*

So I decided to start a company that made more money than my cousin's and to be the CEO, not just the managing director. That became the plan. The negative atmosphere around you can be the motivation to make you succeed. That failure, getting fired at the age of 13, was the big punch I needed to get out there and get my business started.

Now, I encourage and I promote entrepreneurship wherever I go. It's just a fantastic learning process when you're young. When you do something successful as a teenager, you've become an inspiration. Sometimes older people look up to you, instead of looking down on you.

Around the world we have had this recession. People are getting more master's degrees and PhDs, but they're still ending up without a job. It's not that you'll never get a job, but entrepreneurship gives you a Plan B. You create your own route in life.

Q: How do you balance your business with other priorities?

A: It's tough. I had to make a choice about whether I wanted to really focus 100% on my studies, my business, or try to balance both. I went for balancing both. It cost me within my education, but my grades were still relatively good. What I've gained in skill and knowledge has been far superior to letters and grades. When you're taught in school, you're only taught for your test papers. You're not taught outside of the boundaries and I think that's what education lacks around the world. As an entrepreneur, you get to learn those things outside of education: the real, true value of life.

Once you're setting up your own business, you become focused on its success. I kind of gave up time with my friends and family, visiting and playing around. But I still find time to play around. It's not like I need to play around six hours a day. As a young entrepreneur, you've got your own time. So, one day I could work 12 hours and the next I could work for only five minutes. You can balance it out however you want.

There is no deadline that you have to be a multimillionaire by the age of 21. Enjoy the journey; that's the important thing. For each and every person out there, success is different. It's not always about making money and I think that's how I balance it out: I just want to build my life to be something unique and extraordinary.

SABIRUL ISLAM

Q: What challenges have you faced specifically because of your age? How has your age helped you to succeed?

A: If you approach an organization, or a 30-year-old, and say, "Will you give me advice? Do you think I can do this?" they often say, "No – I'm sorry. Who are you?" They have the stereotypical view from TV that teenagers have got their own gang and they're going to make mischief. It's always like that. So, you need to create your own portfolio, your own brand, and make them feel like they're the ones who have to come to you. That is how I built up my business. When I was young, I would always have to go to another person to ask them for help. But now, people are coming to me.

A young person out there who's not just going along with the teenage crew, but who is doing something different in their own way, will stand out. They are the ones who will succeed in life. The younger you are, the more you'll succeed. You're expected to make mistakes: you're young. But if a 30-year-old makes these mistakes, people really crush it. I think what teenagers lack is the belief that they can be unique and extraordinary in life. Make the most of your age because you're not going to be a teenager forever!

> *Sabirul's Favorite Movie:*
> **Terminator 2: Judgment Day**

Q: How have people around you reacted to your success?

A: I've received hundreds of wedding proposals from girls around the world. I don't know how many I should show my parents [laughs]. I'm still only 19, so I don't think I'm ready to get married now. It's quite an insane thing. I've had notes from parents as well, putting their daughters forward. I'll have to pick and study them very well, before I take an offer [laughs].

My cousin is a bit jealous of the fact that I have done more in my life to succeed as an entrepreneur than he has. Now I am the inspiration for him. In that sense, it's quite a blessing.

THE WORLD AT YOUR FEET

He is taking the education route and is studying psychology at university now. So he's doing pretty well for himself.

Every time I see him, I just want to shake his hand and say, "Thank you for giving me this opportunity." The biggest moment in my life was not when I got fired, but when he gave me the opportunity in the first place. If he hadn't done that, I wouldn't have started my first business and I wouldn't have written *The World at Your Feet*. I would probably be working at McDonald's right now.

Q: How did you plan and organize your business?

A: This question gets to the vision for my business: a step-by-step process to nurture a random, ordinary teenager into someone successful. There are so many organizations out there that are just trying to inspire kids. Not enough are actually giving them the opportunity to literally do it with a step-by-step process.

If you put something on a plate for a teenager, they won't think it's of value. They won't think it's something that will help them succeed. If I went out and sold my book to a teenager on the street and said, "This is going to change your life," they would shove the book right into my face.

Teenagers are being taught in school that they have to study and go the educational route. Why not hit them through that route? So, schools have been purchasing my books. Every teenager who reads the book wants to do more. Once they're inspired, they have this drive and motivation to take it to the next level. But you can't succeed as an entrepreneur if you don't know what the business world is about. That's why I created the board game called *Teen-Trepreneur*: it teaches how to market, how to experience a sale, how to expand – anything.

SABIRUL ISLAM

Q: What is the single most important reason for your success?

A: The Three Strikes: the intensity, the integrity, and the intelligence. You need to have the intensity, the strength, to follow your passion. But, in terms of integrity, you have to be honest with yourself as well. Ask, "Is this achievable? Is this something that I really want to pursue in my life?" And then the rest is intelligence.

Q: What would you tell an up-and-coming entrepreneur?

A: Go to TheWorldatyourFeet.com, buy a copy of my book, play *Teen-Trepreneur*, and become a member of the interactive site that I am creating. I think that will be the ultimate way to become a successful entrepreneur. You'll be inspired to make your vision come true, by another teen. You should never forget the name Sabirul Islam.

The biggest mistake that I made was being very arrogant, at one point. I started my first business at the age of 13 and made a lot of money. I even thought about retiring at 14 with the money I had made. The problem with a young person is that once they see that single bit of success, they think that they are the king or the boss.

It only takes one mistake, one form of arrogance, to get other people to look down on you – instead of looking up to you. To rebuild that form of respect might take years. So don't get pride mixed up with arrogance. It's a learning process.

Q: If you had to battle a giant, what weapon would you use?

A: I would use my network. There's a social element within my business that allows me to tackle entrepreneurship and inspire other people. I want to resolve corporate giants by inspiring thousands of young people. I could just ask these customers not to buy or use their services.

Q: What do you want to be when you grow up?

A: I've been growing up in such a deprived community over

the last 19 years. My mom doesn't work. My dad doesn't work. Being the oldest sibling, it's a tough thing. Even whilst we talk, my family is struggling. So, especially in the United States and here in the U.K., where the people are more privileged, I am trying to put that message forth that there are people struggling in Africa and third-world countries.

I want to create a name for myself so that people around the world can look at me and say, "This guy was suffering for his entire life, yet he's done what he's done." Sure, I want to make money. I want to be a millionaire. I want to succeed and enjoy my life. But I also want to help others. For somebody you inspired at the age of 14 or 15 to come back down the road and say, "Wow – you know, you were the person that changed my life" – money can't buy that feeling. That would be the ultimate reward for me.

> *Sabirul's Favorite Book:*
> **The World at Your Feet**
> *by Sabirul Islam*

There will be other things that I pursue along the way. I always want to achieve greater things in life. But, at the end of the day, my vision is to inspire, educate, and create opportunities for young people who are struggling to make something positive happen in their life. There are other things, but I'm not sure what they are yet. I don't want to look too far ahead. The journey is what's happening right now, not what's on the finishing line.

Q: **How did you manage to persevere while your book was being rejected by 40 different publishers?**

A: I was rejected for two reasons. I was 17 at the time. They thought that a 17-year-old couldn't write a book. They also didn't think that there was a market for the book. Let me put it this way: it was stupid – stupid! – of them not to publish my book. It was very naïve. But that's the beauty of entrepreneurship. There could be millions of people out there

SABIRUL ISLAM

who think that your idea is worthless. But it's about the vision you have (that the corporations don't have). You just have to prove them wrong.

In my life, negative factors are actually what have driven me to succeed. Struggle makes me want to prove people wrong. Too many people grow up and don't go to college or university – especially in my culture and community. They take government benefits because it is the easiest way for them to pay for their life. But growing up with that negativity gave me the motivation. Being rejected by those 40 publishers just made me want to prove them wrong.

> **Sabirul's Favorite Website:**
> **Facebook**

So, I self-published the book and the result was huge. If a publisher sells four or five thousand copies of a book, they think that they are a success. My original vision was to sell 100,000 copies. I will one day achieve that. The beautiful thing is that, once I had sold over 40,000 copies, one of those 40 publishers came back and said, "Sabirul, we now want to publish your book." Then, it was me rejecting them.

Q: How did you sell 42,000 copies of your book in nine months?

A: I started in England's schools. I was an ambassador of global entrepreneurship for a network called Enterprise UK. They gave me the opportunity to speak at an event where 250 head teachers were all under the same roof. That was my first ever speaking engagement. It wasn't paid and I wasn't expecting to get anything out of it; I just went there and I told them my story.

Afterwards, around 175 of those teachers came up to me and said, "Sabirul, we'd like you to come speak to our school/college/university – and we'd like 500 or 600 copies of your book for our students." That opened my eyes up to the education sector. Within nine months, I spoke at 373 secondary schools. It was quite the extraordinary thing. That's how I sold the 42,000 books.

Q: Anything else you would like to add?

A: My inspiration is to educate entrepreneurs and help create a platform where they are able to grow in stature and develop their own brands. There may be a few people out there who follow a similar line of vision, but a few is never enough. It's my mission to inspire and create success for both today's and tomorrow's generations.

Website: TheWorldatYourFeet.com
Twitter: @sabirul_islam

"Another fine interview, boys. At 13?! That's awesome. I am curious to know how he decided and picked up web design. Also, must be cool to have girls lining up for him. I say take 'em all!"

**~ Alex M,
Comment on JuniorBiz**

SABIRUL ISLAM

"The best time to plant a tree
is twenty years ago.
The second best time is now."

- Chinese Proverb

15

Freelance Photographer and Beyond
Lindsay Manseau, MyMarriageMarket.com
Portland, Maine

BACKGROUND

Lindsay Manseau's mom started a freelance wedding photography business when Lindsay was 14. She wanted to help her mom out, so she volunteered to accompany her to a bridal show. Two years later, Lindsay had gotten involved in every aspect of the photography business – from networking with brides to doing the paperwork to taking the pictures. She loved every minute of it.

In 2009, Lindsay photographed 25 weddings on her own as a freelancer. Her business was thriving, but she wanted a way to better connect with her couples and the wedding industry. That's when Lindsay began developing My Marriage Market, an online platform where couples and vendors will be able to connect. The site is set to launch later this summer. In the mean time, Lindsay is a 20-year-old college junior studying entrepreneurship and small business at the University of Southern Maine.

INTERVIEW

Q: What would you be doing right now if we weren't talking?

A: Today, I would be editing the first wedding of the season. We photographed it last weekend and I'm really excited to get my hands on those photos. It went amazingly well. The church was huge. We had one person up in the balcony to get wide shots of the whole place. So I can't wait to see them.

Q: What drove you above and beyond, to entrepreneurship?

A: My mom. She started her [photography] business when I was 14 and that's really when I found a love for working and for small business. At her second bridal show, I politely asked her to come along. She said, "Are you sure?" I wanted to help her out in any way I could. I've been doing them ever since and there are very few that I have missed in the past six years. The bridal shows have really encouraged me to break out of my shell and talk to people who I wouldn't normally talk to. It's a lot of fun.

Q: How do you balance your business with other priorities?

A: It's not as easy as I would have thought. My senior year of high school, someone stopped me and asked, "Are you ever not busy?" I thought about it and the answer was, "No." [laughs] I was co-editor of the yearbook along with a whole bunch of other stuff. It just sort of piled on me. I worked 60 hours in the two weeks of graduation, which was probably not the smartest idea. But I like to take things fast-paced and get them done as quickly as possible. So, I don't necessarily balance it all; I just sort of throw it all in there and hope that it works.

Last semester, I crammed five classes onto two days of the week. When you work like I do, you procrastinate a lot. But

> **Lindsay's Favorite Food: Maine Lobster**

procrastination doesn't hold up well when you're going from class to class to class with no time to figure out how far behind you're slipping. So, I sat back this semester and figured out that I can take it slow and still graduate college on time. That way, I make more time for friends, family, and work.

Q: What challenges have you faced specifically because of your age? How has your age helped you to succeed?

A: It has been hard for me to make out-of-the-office connections. These days, people like to meet in places like bars and restaurants to get to know one another casually. In a lot of those cases, I have to say, "I can't go. I'm only 20." It's particularly hard, knowing that I'm that close but still that far. There are also people who look at me like I've got six heads, asking, "How could you know anything?"

But a benefit of being young and naïve is that I don't really care what they think. If they think I'm crazy, that's fine; someone else will think I'm smart. I'm figuring things out as I go along. I try looking at every situation to learn as much from it as I can from it. I'm not at the point where I can say, "I'm smarter than you." I'm at the point where I say, "I'm definitely dumber than you. How can you help me?"

Q: How have people around you reacted to your success?

A: Most people are like, "Great for you! How can I help?" I really like to hear that. Every once and a while, there will be someone who says, "There's no way you could be doing that. Someone else must be doing it for you."

I moved into my first home last July. As a first-time homeowner, I am really experimenting in the kitchen. I had a friend come over who said, "Lindsay, I am so excited to just come over and to see what you're going to cook." To have someone say that really makes me feel like I'm being successful not only in business, but in my personal life as well.

Q: How did you plan and organize your business?

A: I went to the people who could really bring the business in a direction that I wasn't capable of bringing it on my own. I went to the most talented people I know – and that's my family. My team at My Marriage Market is my mother, my twin older cousins, and me.

Between the four of us we've been able to form a company where each person has taken on their own role, making a strong business from the beginning. We started off by writing a business plan and figuring out who was going to do what. My mother has taken on the role of Chief Executive Officer (CEO), myself the role of Chief Marketing Officer (CMO) and my cousins are Chief Financial Officer (CFO) and Chief Information Officer (CIO).

Q: What is the single most important reason for your success?
A: Family. They've been my backbone. My mom took me at age 14 and said, "You can be part of my business. I'll send you to bridal shows. I'll take you to charity events." She let me be a part of every aspect.

I was the one who originally came up with the idea of My Marriage Market, but my family sat down and said, "This is how we can expand upon your idea and really turn it into something that has potential for huge success." It has really been fun to have my family be a part of the project and to respect me as an adult.

Q: What would you tell an up-and-coming entrepreneur?
A: Be strong. Starting your own business is like riding a roller coaster. There are highs and lows and every turn you take is another twist. The lows are really low, but the highs can be really high. You have to be strong, keep your stomach tight, and ride along with the roller coaster that you started.

Don't take no for answer. Not everyone out there has great news to tell you. A lot of people would have you believe that there is no way you could start your own business in this economy. But don't take no for an answer. Say, "You know what? I have the possibility to do it anyway."

There are also a lot of times when you need to listen to somebody else. When you've been through those teen years of thinking that you know everything, it's difficult to be able to sit back and say, "You're right. How can I make myself better?" It's not something that I do perfectly yet, but It is something that I've figured out is important.

Q: If you had to battle a giant, what weapon would you use?

A: I wouldn't battle it with a jackhammer or anything like that. I would probably take its face, put it in Photoshop, and make it pretty. The last thing this world needs is another ugly giant. Then I would just hope it would be happy.

I like to take a situation and make the best out of it. Not every problem is going to turn out to be a pretty giant. You can't beat every giant, but hopefully you can at least make them go away.

Q: What do you want to be when you grow up?

A: At this point, I've given up guessing. I thought that I wanted to be an environmental scientist and I was wrong. I thought that I wanted to be a graphic designer and I was wrong. I ended up in business, so I don't really know where I'm headed to next. I do know that I love small business, entrepreneurship, and the wedding industry. So I hope to do something in those areas.

> **Lindsay's Favorite Book:**
> **A Thousand Mile Walk to the Gulf**
> **by John Muir**

Working in an office is something that always sort of scared me. People who are in the small business industry, specifically the wedding industry, are all so passionate about what they do. But that doesn't really happen in the corporate world. There's something contagious about the small business and entrepreneurship community and I wouldn't leave it for the world.

I would love to see My Marriage Market explode. I really would. It's a heart-felt project that we started to solve a problem in the wedding industry. To have this sort of management tool provided for small businesses will really be a service to the community. So, I would like build My Marriage Market up. After that, we'll see.

Q: What would you tell someone who wants to get started as a freelancer?

A: Get to know people. Build your network from an early age, whether it be with talented friends at school or with classes at a local university. I know that a lot of colleges offer summer courses or camps for young teens. Commit yourself to learning about the industry you're getting into. From there, go to your family and see what kind of support you can get.

Because I was working through my mother's business, I was able to take some of her clients. The first wedding I did [as the lead] was when my mother wasn't able to be the photographer. So, she offered me to the client at a discount and said, "She's a talent, but she's still a relatively new talent." That was over two years ago. It's kind of crazy to think about, because those two years have gone by so fast.

That wedding turned into a friend of a friend's wedding. Then another friend's wedding. The three weddings I

> **Lindsay's Favorite Website: Gmail.com**

did that year, plus all of the assistant work, turned into me marketing myself as a solo photographer. That really took off and I love it. I love every moment I can be there.

To have a network feeding business back to you is really important. This year, we've been trying to ramp up My Marriage Market, so we haven't been doing as many bridal shows. But we have still been getting calls because we have the word of mouth from past clients. I took on so many clients last year and a lot of them have friends and family who are getting married this year. We also have other vendors, venues, and caterers that are recommending us. I guess the whole theme of what I've been saying today is: network, network,

network.

You can try working for someone else. It gives you a chance to build your portfolio and see their level of professionalism. They will teach you how to dress and act appropriately. When you put a professional face forward, you establish your credibility. But it's really hard to be young and be professional all the time, especially with past clients and future clients friending you on Facebook.

Q: How have you moved from a freelance business to a much more scalable online business?

A: My original idea for My Marriage Market consisted of a website solely to find a new way to manage our own clients. It was my family that said, "This is really a solution for the entire wedding industry." It's really going to help the industry by establishing a timeline before the wedding so that couples and vendors know exactly what's going to happen and they can work out all of the kinks before the wedding day. Since my mom started her original business, I think she's had one wedding that stayed on time. This is a way to solve a lot of those issues beforehand.

We started off by establishing a business plan and establishing ourselves with the state. From there, we went to developing a layout for the software. We spent about a week working out all of the kinks of how it was going to be designed. Then we spent another week scrapping all of that and rebuilding it from the ground up, simpler. We sent that off to a developer and had them develop it for us. It had some cosmetic issues. So, we have brought that development in-house and we are moving forward from there.

Development is not nearly as easy as I would have hoped. Finding a really great developer who has as much passion about our project as we do is pretty much impossible. So, to have the ability to bring it back in-house and to move for-

LINDSAY MANSEAU

ward from there is really exciting.

Q: What is the worst situation you've encountered as a wedding photographer and how did you deal with it?

A: The worst situation is when a couple just isn't happy. In one case, we had a couple who booked us for a lot of services, but they had to scale it back when they found out that their family was not willing to pay for everything they wanted. To see someone hurt like that was really a nightmare situation for me. I think every couple has a dream and then they have the reality of what they have in their wallets. We ended up scaling our services back and they were happy with what we could give them.

Q: Anything else you would like to add?

A: Thank you for taking the time to interview me. Check out MyMarriageMarket.com and please be patient because the timetable has really been turned against us.

Website: MyMarriageMarket.com
Twitter: @lindsaymanseau

"My daughter, Sarah, has a love for photography. She followed a professional photographer around for a half-day and watched her shoot senior pictures. Then Sarah volunteered to take senior pictures for a friend. Now I think she's ready to offer her services to a few friends and make a micro business out of shooting senior pictures. Lindsay's interview is an inspiration."

~ Carol T,
Comment on JuniorBiz

MY MARRIAGE MARKET

16

20-year-old Architect Outsourcer
Marshall Haas, Podums, LLC
Dallas, Texas

BACKGROUND

Marshall Haas got his start selling Pokémon cards on the street corner with his friends. But by the time he was 17, Marshall had moved on to architecture. He got a job working for a high-end architect in the Dallas area and began taking classes at a local community college.

Marshall noticed that many architecture firms weren't offering images, or renderings, to their clients. He decided to fill the void by starting his own company, AllRendered, LLC. Marshall recruited a team of 20 artists in the Philippines to create architectural images from floor plans and he began attracting as many as eight clients a month.

Today, Marshall is 20 years old and still working to build AllRendered into a premier rendering service, while pursuing a degree in computer science. He is also in the process of developing a mobile web application called Podums, which will use game mechanics to encourage people to be productive. Whenever he finds the time, Marshall gets his thrills by riding his motorcycles.

INTERVIEW

Q: What would you be doing right now if we weren't talking?

A: Right now, I would be unpacking. I just moved back home with my parents. Any other day, I would probably be out riding my motorcycle. We have sports bikes and super moto bikes, which are really fun.

Q: What drove you above and beyond, to entrepreneurship?

A: I've always had an interest in interesting people who have done remarkable things, whether it's setting records or running amazing companies. Most of these interesting people are entrepreneurs. So, I've always just been interested in doing things differently.

My cousin Ryan is really like a brother or best friend. He got married two weeks ago and I was his best man. Ryan is four years older than me and, when I was 17, he got me into reading business books like *Rich Dad Poor Dad* by Robert Kiyosaki. Naturally, we started a business together. We spent lots of late nights just talking about stuff and working through ideas. That's really what started it all.

Q: How do you balance your business with other priorities?

A: Very carefully. That's part of the reason why I'm leaving my job now. I was doing business, school, work, and I was supporting myself, living on my own. Some things were getting half-done, so I eliminated them. I stopped living on my own and moved back in with my parents. I wanted to focus 100% on a business and that's what I'm doing now.

Six months ago, I realized that I hadn't seen or talked to my riding buddy in two months. There was literally no good reason. So, I had to take a step back and take some time for myself and my friends. My mom talks to me a lot about balance in life. It's sinking in now.

Q: What challenges have you faced specifically because of your age? How has your age helped you to succeed?

A: I'll be straight up: it is harder when people see that you're younger. I have to remember to tell clients, "I'm not a one man shop. I've got a designer and a developer and they're not just my buddies. They're the best at what they do." It's about communicating that I'm not some kid: this is the real deal and we're just as good as the next guy.

There are definitely advantages [to being young]. A computer has been in our lives the entire time we've been alive. That is a big advantage in my industry. I talked [to a client] about social media stuff and he perked up. All of a sudden, it was an advantage that I was young. Now, that company might hire me as a consultant for social media.

> **Marshall's Favorite TV Show:**
> **Family Guy**

Q: How have people around you reacted to your success?
A: I don't consider myself a huge success. I'm nowhere near where I want to be. So, it really doesn't feel like I'm some celebrity or anything like that. I'm not on the front page of *Forbes Magazine*. I don't think that anyone has treated me differently. But it has given me some credibility in business, like when I was looking for sponsors for the BizBreak contest.

Q: How did you plan and organize your business?
A: I didn't use any special resource for teens or anything like that. I read a book and some blogs about how to put together your LLC and structure your company. My cousin has been a mentor with that, as well. Talking to friends and people on the internet who have already done it – that's the best resource that you can get.

[When asked about Podums as a tool] The goal of Podums is to make people more effective in what they do. It merges game mechanics with a task-management application, or a 'to-do' application. You get feedback on what you've done, whether in the form of points, leveling up, or badges. You can use game mechanics to influence your behavior in what you get done, playing it like a game. The working tagline is "Play Your To-Do's."

MARSHALL HAAS

Q: What is the single most important reason for your success?

A: It comes down to execution. It's easy to talk about an idea for a really long time. I did that with my first business: we would just hang out and fantasize about what it would be like to be a business owner. But it's all of the things that aren't attractive, like discipline, that earn you the benefits. You've just got to stop, put your head down, and get to it.

The press loves the whole overnight success thing. It's a misconception. Kevin Rose was featured on the cover of *Business Week* with the headline, "How This Kid Made $60 million in 18 months." But when you look into his back story, you'll see that it was years and years in the making, with him trying all of these different things.

> **Marshall's Favorite Book:**
> **Rework**
> *by Jason Fried &*
> *David Heinemeier Hanson*

Q: What would you tell an up-and-coming entrepreneur?

A: Don't be afraid to try out different ideas. That's where a lot of my experience and insight has come from. But at the same time, you can't treat it like a lottery: "I've got five businesses going, one of them will hit, right?" It doesn't work that way. People are able to build up a business because they focus on one thing. I'm really focused on AllRendered right now and that's why it will take a while for Podums to get built.

Do something that's manageable. If you want to build the next Facebook, but you can't program, it's probably not going to happen. The best thing is to learn to do it yourself. I don't think that being the 'idea guy' works. You either need to have the money to hire someone or you need to learn how to do it yourself. Go build it and you'll learn the whole process.

Q: If you had to battle a giant, what weapon would you use?

A: It's a big giant and I'm just little old me. The only way I could attack it is little by little, but I don't know what weapon I would use. Maybe I would chew off his kneecaps or something like that.

There are advantages to being small. [AllRendered] is extremely agile compared to a big company. If we decide to change course, we can change course at the snap of a finger. So, you start small and then build on progress.

Q: What do you want to be when you grow up?

A: I would like to be the messed-up child of Steve Jobs, Mark Zuckerberg, Bill Gates, and Tim Ferriss – morphed into super-genius entrepreneur. I will probably be a serial entrepreneur and have several businesses. I want to have a family. I would like to break some cool world records. I want to be an interesting person.

It's freeing to be an entrepreneur. Three-and-a-half years ago, I wanted to be an architect. That was the path: in six years I would be a registered architect. Now, I don't know what I'm going to be when I grow up. My life could go anywhere. I've got to meet some cool people like Tony Hsieh, six months before Amazon bought Zappos for 887 million dollars. Entrepreneurship opens a lot of little doors like that, cool opportunities, cool experiences – little stuff. That all adds up.

Q: Why did you turn down a dream internship with one of the fastest growing marketing firms in the country?

A: I thought it would be awesome to work for VaynerMedia for a summer. I really love New York and, mainly, I wanted to absorb Gary and AJ Vaynerchuk's knowledge. So I emailed AJ, explained who I was, and said, "I'm going to be in your city. I would love to grab lunch or whatever." I bought a cheap ticket, got a cheap room with Airbnb.com, and I went up there. At lunch, I told AJ, "Actually, the whole reason why I am here is to meet with you. Here's what I've done..." He seemed pretty impressed and we kept in contact. AJ is a rad

MARSHALL HAAS

dude.

Later, VaynerMedia offered an internship to me, but I guess there was a misunderstanding. I had said that it would have to be a paid internship, because New York is crazy-expensive. But since they are a sought after company, they have the luxury of not paying their interns. AJ told me, "Dude, we've got about a hundred interns applying for this." I was flattered that I was offered the position, but I decided to focus on my business. An internship would give me the skills and experience for my résumé, but working on AllRendered will build my business – something that I own.

Q: You have an outsourced team of 20 designers in the Philippines. How did you get started with outsourcing and how do you continue to manage such a large team?

A: It started with Tim Ferriss' book, *The 4-Hour Workweek*. That's how I was introduced to the whole concept of hiring people overseas. At the same time, I had this architecture job and the main architect had an amazing skill with rendering. I really thought that more firms should offer a visual experience like that for their clients.

> **Marshall's Favorite Website:**
> **sethgodin.typepad.com**

So, I asked a homebuilder for a kitchen floor plan for one of their models. I told them that I wanted to do a rendering for them for free and see how they liked it. I took that floor plan and put up a job on Elance.com and I paid three different companies to do a rendering of it. I ended up going with one of those teams, a group of artists in the Philippines who do watercolors and 3D stills. Then, I just started looking around and contacting architects, saying, "This is what we do."

I've got one point of contact with the team and he manages all of the other guys for me. He's also an architect and one of the artists. I'm the one point of contact for the architects and he's the one point of contact for the renderings. So, I don't have to manage 20 people. It's really easy.

Q: Anything else you would like to add?
A: Whoever reads this, I would love to talk about your ideas. I love bouncing ideas around with people who are also interested in business.

Website: blog.podums.com, AllRendered.com
Twitter: @podums

> "Wow, another talented young kid...hummm...thanks for sharing this and I have learnt something from this interview."
>
> ~ Valentine B,
> **Comment on JuniorBiz**

MARSHALL HAAS

"Being realistic is the most commonly traveled road to mediocrity."

- Will Smith

17

Co-Founder of myYearbook
Catherine Cook, myYearbook
New Hope, Pennsylvania

◆

BACKGROUND

When Catherine Cook and her brother David were growing up in New Jersey, they used to set up little libraries in their house and rent out books to their parents for a small charge. By the time they were in high school, they had launched the social networking site myYearbook.com with a $250,000 investment from their older brother Geoff.

Today, Catherine is a 20-year-old junior at Georgetown University in Washington, DC and myYearbook.com has over 20 million members. Between studying marketing, operations and information management, and psychology, Catherine finds time to take the train up to myYearbook's HQ in Pennsylvania a few times a month. There, 80 employees are working hard to make myYearbook the premier way to meet new people online through ice-breaking games and features. It's working: myYearbook is ranked in the top 25 most trafficked websites in the United States (by comScore) and it pulls in 20 million dollars in yearly revenue.

As co-founder, Catherine keeps busy developing new features and leading myYearbook into the future of social networking. She's also an active myYearbook user and every new member's first friend.

INTERVIEW

Q: What would you be doing right now if we weren't talking?

A: I would be working to develop new Chatter games, since

Chatter is one of our most popular features now. We are getting over a million posts per day [on Chatter]. We try to launch a new feature or extend a feature every two weeks. It's very important to constantly be developing.

Q: What drove you above and beyond, to entrepreneurship?

A: A big part of it was the way that my parents brought us up. We were always taught to be leaders. For instance, if we didn't know what a word meant, we had to look it up in the dictionary. Our parents weren't going to just tell us. It's that kind of thing: do it yourself and find your own path.

One of the things that drove us directly to entrepreneurship was seeing our older brother do it. Geoff, who's 11 years older than me, started a company at Harvard during his sophomore year. At the time, Dave and I were nine and ten. Seeing him have a company, watching it grow, and living with him over the summers in California – it was just such a different environment than our parents' work. The energy was a lot cooler. It was just better. Later, Geoff became our first investor and he stepped in as CEO.

Q: How do you balance your business with other priorities?

A: In general, myYearbook always beats out school. My very first year at Georgetown, I was going to speak at the World Knowledge Forum in Seoul, South Korea. But I had a final that fell smack in the middle of the time I would be there. My international business professor is one of the professors where, if you turn in a paper late, then you fail it – but he said, "You have your own company and you need to do this? Ok." So, I came back, took the exam late, and got an A on it. I've been able to get papers and exams moved in order to fit my schedule better. My professors at Georgetown have been very accommodating.

In my e-commerce class, there were some aspects of the course that would directly relate to social media sites and social networks. So my professor would often look to me to make sure that the numbers were still accurate. My professor would ask me questions like, "Is this website profitable now?" It was an interesting role to play.

> **Catherine's Favorite Movie:**
> **Up**

My high school wasn't the same. For instance, I was going to be in one of New Jersey's newspapers and there was some issue where they didn't want me photographed on school property. So, I went down to the principal's office a few times that week and they would always announce it over the PA system, like, "Catherine Cook, please report to the principal's office." Awkward. But it ended up working out. It's just a different environment. The teachers in the public school system don't have much power. My teachers liked what I was doing, but they had to go with the school's protocol.

Q: What challenges have you faced specifically because of your age? How has your age helped you to succeed?

A: Within two weeks of our launch, we got an offer from a site that was definitely playing on our age. The offer's tone was like, "You're young. You don't know how to do this. Let us do this." It was very negative. We've had things like that from the beginning. But obviously, as we became more successful, comments like that started to drift away.

When I was around the age of 16, we were working to create our 'report abuse' links. Our first meeting was funny, because I had a little bit of trouble getting in. You have to show photo ID and I only had my school ID card (I didn't have a license yet). Then, I walked into the room and there were all of these serious people. There's no way they thought that I would look that young. When you're 16, you look 16. I think it brought a different attitude to the room.

At 20, I don't feel young anymore. There are a lot of people

131

who are doing amazing things at 13 or 14. But a big benefit of [being young] is less stress. I still live at home, so it's not like I wouldn't have a house anymore if something happened to myYearbook. That helps cope with uncertainty. It made it more possible for my brothers and me to take more risks and that's ultimately how you're going to be successful. Obviously, you're going to make some mistakes, but if you're not making mistakes, then you're not making decisions. Being young and having fewer responsibilities makes a big difference there.

Q: How have people around you reacted to your success?

A: It's not like I try to keep a cover, but I don't really talk about it. If I bring it up in conversation, it becomes the conversation. Of course, I love to talk about it. But I don't want to feel like I monopolize the conversation.

My freshman year of college, no one knew except for my best friend. She didn't realize how many hours I put into the site every night. I'm on the site late at night and I also tend to be an early riser. So, when we started living together, she was like, "You never sleep!"

There's a guy who works at our cafeteria, swiping students in. He sees me every day because I eat at the cafeteria. Some time around November, he was like, "You're the girl who created myYearbook, right?" Apparently he's a member. It's fun to meet people who use the site.

Catherine's Favorite Band:
Regina Spektor

I made all of my friends at Georgetown get accounts. C'mon – they're my friends, so they have to support what I do! Now they're on the site all the time. The casual game section is really big with them and at least one of my friends gets on the high score list every week. I can never get onto the high score list! They're really good at it.

Q: How did you plan and organize your business?

A: We mostly followed our gut. We knew that our role was to meet new people, so we obviously had to have a good search tool and a good way to actually view pages. We looked at other sites to get a basic idea of what we liked, what we hated, and what we wanted to do differently. At the time, we didn't know the psychology of page layouts and how people usually scan pages with their eyes. So, we researched some of that information to help us develop. We also had a general sense of how we would make money, through advertising, but we didn't want to focus on that until after we had a million members.

The tiny, tiny amount that Dave and I knew about programming could not have made myYearbook. So, we knew from the very start that we would have to outsource. Luckily, our brother Geoff had connections with people he had networked with through his company. We asked, "Hey – has anyone ever outsourced programming for a website?" and we found a firm in Mumbai for the initial programming. That's how we worked out that first bit.

We launched myYearbook when we were in high school, so our demographic was right there. They were coming up to us in the cafeteria, around the track, and giving us ideas. That started phase two, where we added a lot of breaking-the-ice features to aid in meeting new people.

Q: What is the single most important reason for your success?

A: I work incredibly hard. I don't think that I am especially smart or especially anything – except for diligent. I'm kind of a perfectionist. So generally, if something's not working out, I will stay up until it starts working. I've always been uptight about that, like, "I know it's a small bug, but it's a bug so it's getting out of here."

CATHERINE COOK

For the company as a whole, myYearbook is very open. We have 80 employees but we are very tightly knit. It's a high-energy office, but we all hang out together. We have a bar right next to us and sometimes we'll have an open bar there to celebrate what a good job everyone has done. It's an environment where everyone feels like they know one another.

Q: What would you tell an up-and-coming entrepreneur?

A: To any entrepreneur: if you want to do it, do it now. If you don't, you're going to regret it. So what if you fail? Especially if you're young, the worst that can happen is that you can still put it on your résumé, your college application essay, or a grad school essay. If nothing else, it differentiates you and you'll learn from it in whatever career you end up pursuing.

I've had a few friends who have had ideas about starting a company. They'll talk to me about it because I already did it. But then a lot of them will get cold feet and I don't understand why. They don't have the responsibilities now, so if they're going to do it, they have to do it now.

Q: If you had to battle a giant, what weapon would you use?

A: My first response is magic, but I'm not sure if it counts. Now I'm thinking of *The Big Friendly Giant* by Roald Dahl, so I guess I would stab the giant in the ankle with a brooch.

You could say that the giant is Facebook and Twitter. Being a social network in a Facebook and Twitter world isn't easy. You have to really find your niche and use it. That's the giant's Achilles' heel. Facebook's great for existing social graphs; myYearbook's great for meeting new people. That is why we create all of our applications and social games that get you to meet new people. Facebook doesn't do that. Obviously there's a lot of overlap between Facebook and myYearbook – and that's fine. They can log into Facebook as long as they log into myYearbook too.

Q: What do you want to be when you grow up?

A: It's hard to say. My freshman year of high school, there was no way that I could have known that I would start myYearbook the very next year. I like having that uncertainty. I like not knowing what's going to happen in five years. But, I can't see a job being just a job to me; it has to be a large part of my life. I have to love what I do and I can't do that while working under someone. I have to have creative control and be a leader. So, I definitely think I'm going to continue being an entrepreneur.

myYearbook gave me my love of entrepreneurship. Even though I wanted to be an entrepreneur when I was young,

> *Catherine's Favorite Book:*
> *The Harry Potter Series*
> *by J.K. Rowling*

it wasn't until I was actually working on myYearbook that I really understood what that meant. I have a ton of connections right now. But if it weren't for myYearbook, there is no way that I would be going to conferences and meeting such amazing people. I'm going to continue just because I have these people in my life. I've heard what they've done and I want to do it as well.

Q: Social networking sites aren't easy to get off the ground. How did you know that myYearbook would succeed?

A: I didn't know. With a social network, you need the people; you need the traffic. If you don't have that, then you don't have a company. The best way to [attract people] is to really listen to your customers. What do they want? Once you find that out, then you cater to them. You form a company that fits with what they need. The only thing that really helped Dave and me from the get-go was that we knew our audience better than the other people did. We were launching a website for high school students and being in the same high school as those students really helped.

Now, every level of our company pays attention to the sug-

CATHERINE COOK

gestions that come from the members. I don't think that all companies have their sales team, their QA staff, their developers, and their CEO, CFO, and CTO reading the suggestions. We find out how members are using the site and what we have to do to make it the best experience possible. It's all about listening.

That's why I read all of the comments that people put in my chatter. I spend a few hours each day just looking at the site, looking at our members' profiles, and letting them know, "I'm here. Let me know if you need anything." One time, a member sent me a funny question on one of our chatter games. So, I gave him a high-five, which is one of our ice-breaking features. Within two minutes, he changed his status to, "OMG – Catherine Cook, the founder of myYearbook, just gave me a high-five!" I got a kick out of that.

Q: What's it like to work with your brothers?

A: When you're really close to somebody, there are times when you almost feel like you can read their mind. You can finish each others' sentences. So, a lot of the times there could be miscommunications with other people, but I feel like Dave, Geoff, and I don't really have those instances. We tend to be on the same page. We'll have differing opinions, but when we say something, the others will know what we mean.

Of course, when you're in a family, it could get awkward when you come home. But we have never had anything like that because we separate our work [from family life]. We're all very close and supportive of one another's ideas and we don't take it personally if someone doesn't like an idea. With that said, they did try to throw me in the Delaware one time. They still pick on their little sister.

Q: Why are myYearbook and Facebook still growing while MySpace is struggling?

A: Have you gone to MySpace lately? They're not making it easy to use. And in all of the years MySpace has been around, they've mostly stayed the same. They haven't been dynamic – whereas Facebook and myYearbook have been very innovative. We're always coming up with new features. It's good to be active and to run with your ideas. Like I said earlier, if you're not making mistakes, you're not making decisions. MySpace hasn't been making enough decisions.

I love Facebook. I don't really think of Facebook and myYearbook as direct competitors. If you're going to go on Facebook, that's fine. We just want you to go on myYearbook too. Facebook is for your existing social graph; myYearbook is for meeting new people. Facebook is a great site; myYearbook is a great site. If anything, we're competing for time on site, not necessarily membership.

Since myYearbook is a lot smaller than Facebook, we can learn a lot from what they're doing. I don't say, "Our competitor is doing it wrong – blah, blah, blah." Forget that. If your competitor is a big player, you need to pay attention to what they're doing and learn from it. Otherwise, you're going into the market blind. We plan on becoming bigger ourselves. myYearbook is already the most trafficked site in the comScore teen category and we would like to see that in other categories too.

Q: Anything else you would like to add?
A: If your first idea doesn't work out, just try something new. Tweak the idea a little bit and it could make a world of difference. Go for your goals. Don't let anyone tell you that you can't do it. Lots of people told us that we couldn't: "Three million members? You'll never get that." Now, we have 22 million members. If you have a gigantic goal, you don't have to get all of the way to it to be a major player.

Website: myYearbook.com
Twitter: @cncook

CATHERINE COOK

*"My son is now an 'entrepreneur'.
That's what you're called when
you don't have a job."*

- Ted Turner

18

Voted 'Most Likely to be a Millionaire'
Michael Dunlop, IncomeDiary
South Hampton, United Kingdom

BACKGROUND

Growing up with dyslexia in the United Kingdom, Michael Dunlop never liked school. That didn't stop him from using it to earn big money. As an eight-year-old, Michael sold Pokémon trading cards to his schoolmates – often for ten times the price he paid for them. It was the beginning of a passion for business that earned him a handful of young business awards and his class' vote for 'Most Likely to be a Millionaire'.

At 16, Michael dropped out of school and began to develop websites, including RetireAt21.com. Today, Michael is 21 years old and, though he isn't retired, he is netting six figures a year with his websites. His latest, IncomeDiary.com, has attracted over 10,000 subscribers – all eager to hear Michael's hard-earned advice on how to turn everyday blogs into to profit powerhouses.

INTERVIEW

Q: What would you be doing right now if we weren't talking?

A: I usually take the morning quite easy. I wake up and I briefly look over my emails. I like to see if there have been any commissions. I'll grab a shower and some TV with breakfast. Then I start the day around noon. Perhaps I will do an interview, like I'm doing now. [The early afternoon] is when I am feeling most pumped and full of energy. It's not like I have meetings, so I just do what I like when I like. A lot of my income is passive. I don't like the idea of trading time for money.

139

Q: What drove you above and beyond, to entrepreneurship?

A: I'm dyslexic. I did really badly at school. In England, at 16 we have the basic exam to go on to college (between 16 and 18). I failed my exam, but somehow I had the gift of the gab to get myself in. I didn't want to, but my parents suggested that I should be there because you never know what's going to happen in the future.

> **Michael's Favorite Website:**
> **SmashingMagazine.com**

Eventually, I realized that college was not the place for me and I dropped out. I started working for myself then and I knew that I had to succeed. I had no education. My friends who had no education weren't making much money. They were either living from paycheck to paycheck or they were in debt. It was not something that I wanted to do.

I like computer games and I treat business a bit like a computer game. I count money as points. I'm doing really well: making lots of money and lots of points. I like to beat the competition and treat it more like a game than something serious.

Q: How do you balance your business with other priorities?

A: I didn't have a typical job or go to university like most of my friends, so I could just work when I liked. It wasn't really hard to balance. The only issue was the summers: all of my friends had break. Everyone wanted to go down to the beach and go kayaking. I had to be quite strict with myself or I could have lost momentum.

A lot of things in the blogging business can be run so easily. You set the rules online. You can pre-publish posts. If you have an event to attend, you can publish your post a week before and it will be published while you're there having fun.

Your site can be making money the whole time. I really can't lie to you: there isn't a bad side to my business.

Q: What challenges have you faced specifically because of your age? How has your age helped you to succeed?

A: You've got to hold your own. When I ask to interview these huge names, they'll see that I'm a kid and say, "Why should I do an interview for him? Surely he can't do anything for me." So, you have to put up the benefits before you even speak: "Hey, I have 100,000 visitors here wanting to hear your story. You've got to do this interview."

Now, a lot of people know that young people are coming up with the best ideas and the best sites. So if they don't listen to you, they're a fool. I also think that people trust me more. Online, everyone presumes you want to take their money and then run away laughing. Being young, they think that I'm a nicer person and I don't have intentions of ripping them off. They're right to think that.

I also don't have to push as hard as everyone else. I don't have three kids to pay for. Being young in business is great because you can make mistakes and if everything goes wrong, you can just start again with more knowledge. If you start with nothing and end up with nothing, there's nothing lost.

Q: How have people around you reacted to your success?

A: It's something that I don't really speak about much. Luckily, I built a good base of friends who weren't that interested in money. Still, I would prefer not everyone know. It's funny: I run a whole site about money, but I don't really like to talk about how much I make. I'm not just teaching money, but also lifestyle, mindset and what's really important. The money can help change your life, but you don't need a lot of money to do that.

MICHAEL DUNLOP

Q: How did you plan and organize your business?

A: I really haven't done much of the typical stuff. I haven't read books. I don't read blogs. A lot of it comes down to applying yourself. Too many people give up before they've even started. Listen to Nike: just do it. Clearly, they know what they're talking about.

There's a quote that I like: "Entrepreneurship is living a few years of your life like most people won't, so that you can live the rest of your life like most people can't." Work hard now and you can do whatever you like for the rest of your life.

Q: What is the single most important reason for your success?

A: I packaged my content and my business in a different way. A lot of people copy. What I do is copy all the good things from all of the different businesses and put them into one amazing thing. You've got to stop doing all the things that people have tried, tested, and found out don't work. Apart from that, you want to surround yourself with great people, great minds, and get yourself a mentor.

Q: What would you tell an up-and-coming entrepreneur?

A: I want to re-emphasize my point: start and then do it. Lots of young entrepreneurs don't start and they don't do it. Educate yourself more, learn more, and get a mentor. Diversify. You want to have different things going on so that if one fails, you will have something else to fall back on. Don't keep all of your eggs in one basket.

Q: If you had to battle a giant, what weapon would you use?

A: I'm not someone who would want to kill him, so I couldn't use a gun or an axe. I would set a trap with some rope and sort of use my knowledge. A lot of times winning is just about having more common sense than the competition.

I think that's something I apply to business. With IncomeDiary, you can subscribe or you can click on an affiliate link. I give you two options. Either way I make money. I don't give you the choice to go to a friend's site or to some advertiser. It's called the no-leakage rule. Then, if I get you in my funnel system, I give you lots of great tips and updates. I give you a lot more than anyone else would. It's like you become my friend. Perhaps I would do that with the giant. After a while, I could use him to do something for me. I could sell him something.

> **Michael's Favorite Movie:**
> **Groundhog Day**

Q: What do you want to be when you grow up?

A: It doesn't really come down to a job, money, or anything like that. Like everyone else, I just want to be happy. At first, I wanted to be a billionaire – and I know I could be if I wanted to. But if you're a billionaire, your kids could get kidnapped for ransom money or something like that. I just want a simple life. I think that I would be happy running a small business and helping people. That's the whole point of IncomeDiary: not to get filthy rich, but just to get by, be happy, and help other people.

I have ideas for some really big businesses, one being an extreme sports business. But that's more for me, because I want the fun of doing extreme sports and being involved in the industry. This year I want to create a couple of projects and maybe write a book. Maybe in a year or two, I will steer away from the business. I just take every day as it comes.

Q: What has been the impact of personally meeting some of the top internet entrepreneurs – such as Gary Vaynerchuk, Yanik Silver, Carrie Wilkerson, and Bob Parsons?

A: Some of it is confidence. You feel like, if you're friends with these guys, there's nothing to be afraid of talking to anyone else. A lot of it is power by association. If you're friends with one person, you're friends with the others. We [internet entrepreneurs] all have the same interests. We all want to work hard, make lots of money, and then enjoy it. So a lot

MICHAEL DUNLOP

of us click really well. They've also taught me plenty, recommended me to people, and opened doors for me. But I'm not friends with anyone just because of what they can do for me.

You can't always get a real connection over the internet. I have some good friends online, but it's different. Putting a face to someone really helps. It makes networking a lot easier. I don't sell myself too well on the internet, because I'm really laid-back and I don't really want to hype myself up. But at events, I get to meet loads of great people really quickly and I can call them friends because I've met them face to face.

> **Michael's Favorite Band:**
> **Lionel Richie**

When I got into the business, a lot of people gave me a lot of their time and they helped me out. Now, I like to do the same for other people. It's a trait that you see in a lot of entrepreneurs. So you usually don't have to have much traffic to interview someone. Then, once you've got that first connection with an interview, it's really easy to keep that relationship going. I would call most of my interviewees friends.

Q: How would you build a business in a world without internet?

A: There are so many things that I've thought about doing. It just depends on how much money you start with. If I didn't have much money, I would probably start with travel, like a taxi business. I would try to make it nationwide. Once I had taxis, I would do buses, boats, ferries, and planes and become known as the only source for travel. I can do something small, but it has to be big. That doesn't make much sense to most people, but it's true.

Q: Anything else you would like to add?

A: Especially with blogging, there is practically no risk. It's about eight bucks for a domain and you get your first month of hosting for about a cent. So, give it a few months. If you fail, you're down $25, maximum. There's no better feeling than knowing that you don't have to rely on anyone for money.

Everyone out there, if you are starting off and you need a hand or just want a question answered, you can contact me or just check out my forum. Get in there and start.

Website: IncomeDiary.com, RetireAt21.com
Twitter: @michaeldunlop

> *"Great interview, Nick. I'm personally a big fan of Michael as he's not only a great entrepreneur but also a really nice guy. It's clear that he gives more value to his readers than 99.9% of bloggers out there. Keep up the good work Michael and Nick!"*
>
> **~ Simon R,**
> **Comment on JuniorBiz**

MICHAEL DUNLOP

"Vision without action is a daydream.
Action without vision is a nightmare."

- Japanese Proverb

19

From 'Mow Boy' to $135K
Emil Motycka, Motycka Enterprises
Longmont, Colorado

◆

BACKGROUND

Emil first flirted with business when he was in the first grade. Living across the street from a golf course provided a free and steady supply of stray golf balls. He would collect the golf balls, wash them off in his mother's sink, and then sell them near the fairway for a dollar a pop. By the time he was in the eighth grade, at 13-years-old, Emil had taken out his first loan: $8,000 to purchase a commercial lawn mower. He paid the four-year loan off in two years.

It was the beginning of Motycka Enterprises, LLC – a company that currently provides work for about 65 people in Northern Colorado. Motycka Enterprises offers everything from building and janitorial maintenance to lawn care, tree care, snow removal, and even Christmas light installation. The company helped Emil earn $135,000 his senior year of high school. Emil is currently a senior at the University of Colorado's Leeds School of Business in Boulder, CO.

INTERVIEW

Q: What would you be doing right now if we weren't talking?

A: I love to sleep. If I wasn't sleeping, I would be online looking at things that I could do to enhance my business – like new lines of service or new equipment that would improve production. If it wasn't online, I would be reading a book. I love to read about what other people did and learn from them; I can learn countless lessons, both good and bad, from an

147

autobiography of a successful businessperson.

Q: What drove you above and beyond, to entrepreneurship?

A: When I was in third or fourth grade, I had a teacher who wanted us to explore career paths. At that time, being an adult was so far away. The career I wanted was just whatever I thought would be really cool. Since I liked big machines and being outside, I wanted to be a landscaper. She kindly pointed out that a landscaper wasn't a career; it was a job. I ended up doing my project on being a landscape architect.

> *Emil's Favorite Band: Lady Gaga*

But in the process of doing the paper, I learned a lot about the landscape industry and saw the potential money to be made in mowing lawns. $10 a lawn would make me $20 per hour. None of my friends made that much. When I was asked by my aunt and uncle to mow their lawn, I didn't think twice – the rest is history.

Q: How do you balance your business with other priorities?

A: I've never really thought of it as a balancing act. I always put school first and business second, as best I could. But there were days when I would miss school because I would be out scooping snow all night and I would just be too tired to go to school.

This hit me hard my freshman year at college, when there was a blizzard during finals week. One of the hardest things for me to do was to call up my customers and tell them that I wouldn't be able to do the work for them. I promised it would never happen again. I was forced to learn and understand the business of sub-contracting. Through that process, I learned the power of hiring out to people underneath you.

Maybe I haven't done as well in terms of putting aside set time for friends and family. When there would be a family event, like a dinner, I would always get there – but not usually on time. My family understands and my friends respect that work is important to me. Unfortunately, there are times when I haven't been able to go to a party or an outing because of my priorities.

Q: What challenges have you faced specifically because of your age? How has your age helped you to succeed?

A: When I was younger, everybody thought that it was cute. I just had to show up and they would say, "Mow my lawn." When I was in high school, people questioned, "Should I let this teenager on my property?" They didn't really trust that I would do the job. Through that, I learned the importance of building trust with the customer. Initially, they are hiring you for the price. But after you form that relationship, they are hiring you for you – and that is what gives your company value.

Starting when I was young helped, because at that time I didn't have to worry about money. So I wasn't really afraid to fail. I didn't even think of failing. When you are young, you have that fresh perspective on life and an innocence towards business, because money isn't really what's important to you. I mean, when I first started, my mom was still tucking me in at night. When you are older, you worry about how you are going to fail. You almost plan it out. In a way, a business plan is like a 'here's how to not fail' plan. I never thought of failing. I never had a plan. I only thought, "What am I going to do next?"

Q: How have people around you reacted to your success?

A: When I was younger, even though they respected my work, my friends would say, "What are you doing this weekend? Still mowing those lawns, huh? Well, that stinks because we're going to the pool this weekend and you should come... but you can't." It eats at you after a while.

But it turned around when I got older and could drive. I could choose, "Which one of my five trucks do I want to drive to school today?" It's nice when you actually have your own money to take girls out on dates – not allowance money mommy and daddy gave you.

For my family, I know that I have made them proud. My parents let me chart my own course with the business as long as I was enjoying it. They weren't going to step in and intervene. So I haven't seen any special treatment, except when I need a little bit of financial help. Since they are both entrepreneurs, they know what it takes to run a business and they aren't going to sugarcoat it. They aren't going to feel sorry for me when I have to work long hours.

Q: How did you plan and organize your business?

A: There are a lot of things that I could have done that I didn't. All I know is that if I had a loan, I would make sure that the payment got made no matter what. If that meant not taking any money for myself to make sure that the business got taken care of, I would do that. I don't really pay myself. To me, it's really more of learning experience. It's more about finding the next step, how to get there, and what it's going to cost.

Q: What is the single most important reason for your success?

A: I think it's my good looks [laughs]. Actually, I think we'd be bankrupt if we put it on that. The real answer is work ethic and determination. If the job's not done then it's not done, but it will be done before I quit. I only leave a job once it meets my standards – and I have very high standards, being OCD to a degree.

Although I love it, sleep is for the weak. I sleep four hours a night on average. There's never enough time. If I'm doing something unproductive, it might be fun in the moment, but I feel like I wasted that time and I can never get it back. That's okay every so often, but I would rather put that time and energy into something more productive.

I have heard that the best learning environment isn't one in which you're given the answer, but one in which you're given the environment to learn the answer. Entrepreneurship provides a really good environment, but without answers. So if something works, I'll keep doing it. If not, I'll have to adjust. There's so much to learn about business and how it works, its impacts and potential, so it's a fascinating field to study. I see entrepreneurship as the most exciting career path. It's limitless – financially, intellectually, and socially.

Q: What would you tell an up-and-coming entrepreneur?

A: First, go and do what you love to do. If you're not into it, it's not going to be any fun. You're definitely not going to want to stay up all night to get it done – and you will have to pull all nighters routinely. Secondly, don't let people tell you that you can't do it. Just look them in the eyes and tell them "thanks" and that you value their opinion. Then use it as fuel to prove them wrong.

> *Emil's Favorite Book:*
> **E-Myth**
> *by Michael E. Gerber*

Finally, start today, not tomorrow. If anything, you should have started yesterday. Just like investing, the earlier you start, the more time you have to mess up. Don't consider messing up to be a failure. The biggest failure you can have in life is not trying at all. You're not risking anything by trying, especially if you are young. Go try – and don't look back. Just have fun. The money will come.

Q: If you had to battle a giant, what weapon would you use?

A: I would use words. Martin Luther King, Jr. has always been a role model for me in terms of his determination and belief in non-violence. I don't like to fight; I'm especially not big in the muscle department. Having a mom who is a lawyer, I learned

EMIL MOTYCKA

from an early age how you can use words to your advantage rather than fighting it out. That way, both people win. It might not be as fast or direct as a battle, but you might make a friend out of it.

Q: What do you want to be when you grow up?

A: I have at least another year left of college. After that, I would like to either take some time off and work on my business or stay in the school mindset and work on an MBA or a law degree, just for fun.

> *Emil's Favorite TV show:*
> **The Office**

Eventually, I would like to get in the real estate market on the development side – property management and investment. In my business, all of the equipment is losing value on a daily business. I call it an asset depreciation business. If you buy equipment today, it will be worth very little after daily use in 30 years. Whereas, real estate is an asset appreciation business. If you buy property today for a million dollars, it could easily be worth five million dollars when you retire in 30 years.

Q: What would it take to earn $1,000,000 by the age of 25?

A: It would take a ramp-up in my mowing operations to build a larger clientele list, which I could then solicit for additional work (like Christmas light installation in the winter, lawn aeration in the spring, or sprinkler system blowouts in the fall). If I could get a couple hundred more clients under my business, I could hit that mark within three to five years.

Q: Anything else you would like to add?

A: I didn't think of what I did as being an entrepreneur until I won some awards and that funny word happened to be in the title. I think kids need to not be afraid of the word 'entrepreneur'. It took me a while just to learn how to spell it.

What I've done isn't hard. Anyone can do it. I'm not a genius,

MOTYCKA ENTERPRISES

nor do I come from a wealthy background. I've built my business from the ground up and today it's my baby, a child I am hoping to raise to serve as my retirement account when I get older – much like my mom's plan for me [laughs].

I know a lot of people who have a job that pays the rent but they hate going to it and so they don't ever become good at doing it. I have other friends who love what they do and then it never feels like work. If you keep that in mind, then the money is never going to be an issue. There are a lot of people who think, "What job can I do to make a 100 grand a year?" But going into entrepreneurship as a young person is great because it gives you a lot of flexibility and you learn about yourself and others.

Entrepreneurship is a calling: you either want it or you don't. It's a roller coaster ride that has its lows and highs but it's an adventure you'll never regret. You learn things you can't learn at school or on the streets. If you follow your dreams, you can have a lot of fun doing it. But if it's forced on you, like by a parent, it's never going to be fun.

Lastly, never forget to thank those who help you. Being young, you don't have much to offer besides a 'thank you'. With that, I would like to thank my parents for their support and encouragement, my third/fourth grade teacher for introducing me to a new way of thinking, my aunt and uncle for asking me to mow their lawn, my mentors and advisors, and all of my customers over the years for their support, guidance, and tolerance of my business ventures.

If anyone wants to learn how to start a mowing business, feel free to send me an email and I will do what I can to help you out.

Website: motyckalawns.com
Twitter: @emotycka

EMIL MOTYCKA

"Every generation needs a revolution."

- Thomas Jefferson

20

Co-Founder of World Entrepreneurship Day
Lauren Amarante, World Entrepreneurship Day
Tempe, Arizona

◆

BACKGROUND

Lauren Amarante is a born leader. When she was nine years old, she used to get all of her friends to join together after school and sell sandwiches, Oreos, and lemonade. From elementary school to high school, Lauren was a perennial class president and team captain. Then, when her high school basketball coach was diagnosed with breast cancer, Lauren helped plan and organize an event to raise money for a cure, which has become a yearly fundraising event.

Later on, as a sophomore at Arizona State University, Lauren co-founded World Entrepreneurship Day (WED). WED's first celebration of entrepreneurship, in 2009, was a huge success: 22 countries around the world participated. Since then, WED has partnered with the United Nations to scale its successful model around the world. The 2010 WED was kicked off at the United Nations Headquarters in New York City and celebrated in over 35 other countries around the world. Speakers included Marc Ecko (founder of Marc Ecko Enterprises), Beth Comstock (CMO, GE), and Maria Bartiromo (of CNBC's *Closing Bell*).

Lauren is going to be a senior this fall at ASU. She plans to continue growing World Entrepreneurship Day and inspiring people around the world to action.

INTERVIEW

Q: What would you be doing right now if we weren't talking?

A: Right now, I should be studying for the GMAT exam. I'm applying to Harvard Business School's 2+2 MBA Program. Basically, it invites college juniors to apply early and, if they get accepted, they're guaranteed a spot in three years. Given my future plans for WED, Harvard Business School's global network and case study method will help develop my global knowledge and my problem solving skills.

Q: What drove you above and beyond, to entrepreneurship?

A: I didn't even know what the word 'entrepreneur' meant until I was a freshman in college. Once I learned about the world of entrepreneurship, I knew, "This is for me." Before that, I was always working hard on school events and being president of this club or that. I was really ambitious and passionate about leadership. For me, starting my own company or a non-profit organization was really just the best use of those traits.

There was a friend of mine who was involved in a CEO (Collegiate Entrepreneurs Organization) club at Bryant University, where I used to attend. Once I got into that club, it was a roller coaster ride. I began consulting for start-up entrepreneurs, where I got to see the challenges that they faced. Eventually, I felt like I was good at advising them and that it was time to do my own thing. That's how I got started.

> *Lauren's Favorite Band:*
> *Billy Joel*

Q: How do you balance your business with other priorities?

A: I'm still trying to find out the answer to that one. The accomplishments of WED have come at huge sacrifices in other areas of my life. I have just had to forgo going out or spending all of my time outside in the Phoenix sun. It's also really hard to stay healthy and work out when you have a million things on your plate. Homework has been a struggle, but I'm able to pull it off. Balance, for me, has become completely dependent on discipline, focus, and organization.

When it comes to balance, family and friends has been the most difficult aspect of my life. I've found that it's all about setting expectations. For example, when I go home to live with my family for the summer, I tell them, "When you're gone for the workday, I'll be working all day. Then you can expect me to be available the full evening." So, when it's 5:30 pm and the family comes home, the laptop gets closed. That has been really hard, because there are a ton of things that I could do to add more value to WED. But, I wouldn't be here right now if it weren't for my family. They are not entrepreneurs in any sense, but they are incredibly supportive. I need to show that I appreciate them.

The same standard should be held for your friends. But in the college dorm setting, it is harder because you're with them all the time. If you own a company, you're going to have to say, "Sorry, can't," a lot every weekend. You'll learn, though, that certain friends are good for you and certain friends are not good for you. The good ones will understand that if you don't see them for a week, it's not because you don't care for them. You're just busy. I have found a few friends who – even if I don't see them for a month – as soon as we get back together, it's like we had just hung up on the phone.

Another big lesson has been saying 'no'. Many interesting projects have presented themselves to me as a result of WED, but if I said 'yes' to even half of the opportunities, there's no way that I would get to accomplish everything I want to for next year's WED.

Q: What challenges have you faced specifically because of your age? How has your age helped you to succeed?

A: Honestly, I cannot think of one challenge. I am so happy that I am doing this stuff while I'm so young. In fact, most of the opportunities that come up are because of my age. For example, I met most of the people that spoke at our United Na-

LAUREN AMARANTE

tions event at conferences that I was able to attend for free, because I was a college student. These speakers flew out to the event on their own dollar and moved their crazy schedules around – because they believed in World Entrepreneurship Day's mission, but also (I believe) because I am a college student. I was also able to approach different organizations within my school to get grants to cover my travel expenses.

Advice is huge. Anyone will give advice to a college student. Right now, we're investigating how to grow WED, how to scale it, and how to make sure the brand is what we want it to be. These are big, big questions – and I can turn to almost anyone and ask their advice, usually for free. It is, however, generally a good rule to try to buy them lunch to show that you really care.

I'm going to be kind of sad when I graduate, because I know that there is no better time to start a company than when you're young. You have no responsibilities, other than your homework. You only have to feed your own mouth.

Q: How have people around you reacted to your success?

A: Other than my grandmother bragging to her friends? It's almost like my parents expect these things. So, when I tell them about anything new that I'm working on, they're like, "Well, of course you are!" My dad and my step-mom work for an insurance company, so they're extremely risk-averse. They're always providing advice from a viewpoint that I would have never considered. As each year goes by, and I continue on a path of success, my parents just keep returning support.

Q: How did you plan and organize your business?

A: We did not use a business plan. We basically turned to the whiteboard and started picturing what it could be. Typically at a university, the janitors will be cleaning all of the classrooms from 9:00 pm on. So, I would go to [an ASU building] and literally take over an entire classroom to plan. Each room has 10 or 12 whiteboards. Today, I have hundreds of photo images that I've taken of my whiteboards, writings, and plans.

There has been a lot of experimenting as well. We've been trying different ways to grow WED through social media for two years. Eventually, we found a way that actually kicked off and inspired more events. One of our country champions (who are kind of like the leaders of the different countries that run the events) got 500 fans on Facebook in a few days.

> **Lauren's Favorite Book:**
> **Purple Cow *by Seth Godin***

Q: What is the single most important reason for your success?

A: Mentorship. I have focused on surrounding myself with people who have amazing experience and can be great mentors. Most college students, myself included, have a clouded vision of the world. Certain mentors can just open it up and show you something completely different.

It has also been sheer hard work and determination. Once you get that vision down, it's all about execution. You could have a million ideas, but they're all worthless if you don't get them done.

Q: What would you tell an up-and-coming entrepreneur?

A: If the slate were wiped clean and I had to start over, I would first figure out what area I'm interested in – be it technology, leadership, entrepreneurship, science, or whatever. Then, I would relentlessly seek out mentors. One creative way to do that is to approach someone in your industry who is leading the way. Then offer to work on a project for them and do it for free. You will be amazed by how much you'll learn and the mentor that you'll get out of it. I did that this past semester with Dan Ariely, author of *Predictably Irrational* and the newly-launched *Upside to Irrationality*; Dan is an industry giant in the field of behavioral economics.

LAUREN AMARANTE

Another piece of advice I would give to young entrepreneurs: if you're not in an uncomfortable situation every single day, then you're doing something wrong. It could be approaching someone and asking for funding or asking your boss for a raise – those types of uncomfortable things. If they come through, they're going to add huge value.

Lauren's Favorite Movie:
Avatar

Young entrepreneurs need to nail down the art of networking. Some of my best opportunities have come out of those cold-call approaches. I remember last year, I was approaching Matt Groening, the creator of *The Simpsons*, at the EG conference. I was so star-struck that I was shaking, thinking, "Oh – this guy is a legend!" But you just have to make it happen.

Young people in general must realize that there will be no better time to start a company than right now – particularly while in college. Don't let this be a missed opportunity. School activities are great. In fact, I attribute a lot of my success to being involved in school activities when I was young. I was president of the class, running the proms, etc. – which is parallel to what I'm doing now (producing events). But there comes a point when it's time to move away from the school stuff and start investigating the real world. Who says you have to wait until the day after you graduate?

Lastly, I see a lot of students who want to start a company, but they are too afraid of quitting whatever school activities they are involved in. I've learned a simple, but powerful lesson in that area: you can't make everyone happy – and you shouldn't try to. There are only 24 hours in a day. Starting a company, or anything new for that matter, requires some necessary sacrifices.

Q: If you had to battle a giant, what weapon would you use?

A: I would pull a rope tight to make him fall. It relates to my business because I like to sweep people off of their feet. I value perfection, excellence, and the surprise factor.

Q: What do you want to be when you grow up?

A: Recently, the president of Arizona State University came to our class and showed us how to create our own personal vision. Mine is educating, connecting, and celebrating entrepreneurs around the world through revolutionary online platforms and extraordinary experiences. That combines the things that I am most passionate about: mentoring people, educating people, and then creating these celebratory experiences. I really don't know what I want to *be* when I grow up, but that's generally what I want to be doing.

More specifically, I want WED to turn into a larger organization with a goal that is pretty parallel to my personal vision. Picture the impact that would result from a combination of education, conferences, and mentorship opportunities for our country champions and their communities.

Q: What was the very first thing you did after you thought of World Entrepreneurship Day?

A: It started with an entrepreneurship day at my university, which was really successful. The first thing I thought of after was, "I wonder if there is a worldwide one?" I went to Wikipedia and looked it up. If there had already been a world entrepreneurship day, I wouldn't have wanted to mess that up by doing the exact same thing. Thrilled to discover that there wasn't already one, the first thing that I did was call a mentor of mine and he ended up being the co-founding advisor. Troy [Byrd] has had an incredible impact.

If I hadn't reached out to mentors before I got the idea for WED, then I wouldn't have had anyone to call. So, before you even get the idea, be out there building your network. A

LAUREN AMARANTE

huge supporter of WED, Rob Ukropina from Black Diamond Ventures in Los Angeles, says, "Your network is your net worth." The quality of the people who can help you is really your net worth.

Q: WED is a global event. How do you coordinate everyone?

A: We use a ton of online tools, all free, like Google Forms. Our country champions fill out an online form every couple weeks that asks for their progress: have you secured any new press this week for your WED event? Have you signed on any new speakers? Etc.

We also have office hours on Skype. They're always at awkward times, because most of our members are sleeping right now. I have to wait until they're awake, which is usually in the AM of the night. Then they can just call us and talk to us about any of the challenges they are facing.

I can't tell you how much impact Facebook has had on WED. We had all of our country champions set up their own Facebook fan pages, added them as admins, and created really beautiful profile pictures. All of the country champions became friends and then started commenting and sharing advice with one another. It really has lifted a lot of the pressure off of my shoulders. The future of education will look like that, with groups of "students" working together and actually teaching each other.

For one example, our country champion in Singapore created this great promotional video for their WED event in less than a day. They posted it on Facebook, and before we knew it, the Phillipines started creating a video and then Ghana started creating a video. Social media has had an exponential impact.

We are also planning on recording instructional videos. This year, we really started to grasp all of the common challenges between the country champions: sponsorship, marketing, logistics, and speakers. There is an amazing entrepreneurial incubator at ASU called SkySong. It's world-class. We plan to basically just go up there and answer some live webcast questions [about the common challenges] and put the videos up on our site.

> **Lauren's Favorite Website:**
> **sethgodin.typepad.com**

My favorite part about World Entrepreneurship Day is mentoring budding entrepreneurs all over the world. Growing up in America, a lot of young people are ignorant to global cultures. I was most amazed when I learned that, no matter their geographical location, many young entrepreneurs out there have very similar ambitions, desires, and interests. It's inspiring.

Q: Do you ever wish you were a normal college student?

A: Not at all. Normal is boring. I'm at ASU – the most known party school in the country – so temptations are an inevitable piece of the pie. But for me, that's just one sacrifice that I've made for something that is much more worth it. I would honestly more enjoy spending a Friday night working on WED than doing anything else in the world. This being said, it goes back to your previous question: it's all about balance. You need to find that fun time or you'll just go nuts!

Plus, the more you contribute now, the better quality of life you'll be able to achieve in the future. There is a great quote: "Entrepreneurship is living a few years of your life like most people won't, so that you can spend the rest of your life like most people can't." Some of the entrepreneurs [in this book] are 20-year-olds who have started 20 million dollar companies. To me, capital is freedom. Who on Earth would want to be normal when you could have that type of freedom?

Q: Anything else you would like to add?

A: Definitely start something now. Whether it's small or it's big, whether it's a company or a student club, whether it's a failure or success – start *something*. It's all about failing hard and failing fast. Obviously your goal is not to fail, but it's better to fail now and reap all the inherent lessons, than to sit back and do nothing. Even if you eventually go on to work for someone else, future employers will appreciate your early entrepreneurial endeavors because they tangibly demonstrate execution, initiative, and leadership.

Website: WorldEshipDay.com
Twitter: @lafactor

> *"I would have to agree with Lauren's point of view about putting in the work now. Giving up the partying and the typical student life is really only a minor sacrifice in comparison. I too would much rather spend my friday nights at my desk working hard on my projects. I enjoy it, as does any entrepreneur that really believes in their work.*
>
> **~ Daniel M,
> Comment on JuniorBiz**

21

5-Month Sprint to 6-Figure Internet Success
Alex Maroko, Game Speed Insider
East Lansing, Michigan

BACKGROUND

As a 13-year-old, Alex Maroko was cut from his basketball team. At 15, after years of practicing training techniques, Alex became a freelance athletic trainer. As word of mouth spread, the clients rolled in. After graduating high school, Alex moved from Michigan to Tampa Bay, FL, where he played Division II basketball at Eckerd College. That's also where he decided to take his business to the next level.

In early 2009, Alex went from training clients in person to doing everything online. His first product was a speed training system called *The Truth About Quickness*. It earned $20,000 in the first week of its release. In the six months since, Alex has been developing more websites and products, along with an online coaching program. Today, Alex is 21 and Game Speed Insider, his athletic training business, is going stronger than ever. He's also pursuing a kinesiology degree part-time at Michigan State University.

INTERVIEW

Q: What would you be doing right now if we weren't talking?

A: Right now, I would actually be studying for this big anatomy exam that I have tomorrow. I'm glad that we chose the interview for this time so that I have an excuse to take a break. But on a normal day, I would be working online. At this time, around three or four in the afternoon, I would probably be working on my emails, my auto-responder, or something.

Q: What drove you above and beyond, to entrepreneurship?

A: I don't know where it comes from, but I have always had this burning desire to be different than everybody else. I don't have an unbelievable desire to make a lot of money, have a huge business, or become really well-known. In fact, if everyone around me was starting their own businesses, I probably would have been like, "Screw that! That's the last thing I want to do." But instead, I saw everyone around me playing videogames, sleeping in, and going to parties. So, I found something that was productive and good for me financially.

> **Alex's Favorite Website:**
> **ClickBank.com**

So that's how I got started, but once I was in, I was completely sucked in. From that point on, it's just desire to grow, build, and never stop learning.

Once I decided that this was what I was going to be doing, then it was what I was going to be doing. There wasn't any other option. There weren't any obstacles either. It was just an open road that I was going to take. Entrepreneurs are a very rare breed. Not everyone is an entrepreneur. But when you find one, you can spot them.

Q: How do you balance your business with other priorities?

A: I become fixated on something and then it's all I think about. Especially in the beginning, when I first started with my online business, I would spend hours and hours every single day doing nothing other than work on my business. I would wake up, a full-time student, and go to classes. Then, when I got back to my apartment, I would close that door and work like a mad scientist for hours and hours. I didn't go out. I didn't really hang out with my friends for a couple of months. It was just business, business, business.

Yanik [Silver] used an analogy and it really hit home for me. A

GAME SPEED INSIDER

business is like a rocket ship: it takes a ton of work to get off the ground, but once you get off of the ground a little bit, it becomes a lot easier. You just start flying. So, now that I am at this point, I really feel like I've got a good balance with everything and my priorities are straight. I get to go out. I hang out a lot with my friends. Yesterday, on a whim, I decided that I wanted to go to Florida for four days. So I bought a plane ticket and I'm going there tomorrow. I have the ability to do things like that now.

On a side note, I was a full-time student up until this semester and I had to cut it down so that I could spend some more time on my business. It has been – I don't want to say it has been impossible, because I don't necessarily think anything is – but it has been really tough. Taking 15-16 credits of 300/400 level classes and trying to manage a full-time online business really took its toll on me. Now that it is part-time, I can focus on the business. It continues to grow and my productivity has shot through the roof.

Q: What challenges have you faced specifically because of your age? How has your age helped you to succeed?

A: The number one issue I had coming in, specifically in my niche, was the credibility factor. How can someone who's 20 years old be an expert at training? But there are lots of different things that you can do to increase your credibility. I reframed the public view on me: instead of being a 'young person', I'm a 'prodigy'. You can take one thing that's negative and you flip it around and frame it however you want.

[As a 21-year-old,] I've got a ton of energy. You can probably hear it when I talk. My mind moves a million-and-one miles an hour. So, I have this never-ending thirst to succeed and to make a lot of things happen. An older person may have worked a couple different jobs and been rejected a few times, but I don't have that in my mind. I don't have the fear that it might not work out. I guess it's kind of ignorant of me;

ALEX MAROKO

I don't know any better. All I know so far is success, so those negative thoughts never really enter my mind.

Q: How have people around you reacted to your success?

A: My good, close friends laugh about it. They think it's funny. They all call me 'The Truth' now, based on *The Truth about Quickness*. Everyone around me is really supportive and excited for me. But a lot of people don't understand it. My mom always asks me what she's supposed to say when a friend of hers comes up and asks, "How is Alex making all of his money? How did he buy that car? What does he do on-line?" She just doesn't know how to explain it. She's a smart woman; don't get me wrong.

I get recognized when I go out in public. It's funny. People just come up to me and say, "Hey – you're Alex Maroko, aren't you? You're awesome." I even had one kid who asked me to sign an autograph for him. I never thought that would actually happen. So, it's cool.

Q: How did you plan and organize your business?

A: On December 29th, 2009, I invested about $100 in a really, really good calendar/planner. Every Sunday night, I basically plan out my entire week and write down every single thing that I need to do for my business. I don't write everything, but I plan maybe three or four hours of work each day for my online business. Once it's on paper, I feel like I have to do it. So, regardless of what else is going on in my life, that always makes sure that I am getting done what I need to get done.

But the main reason I got the planner was just so that I could tell people in interviews that I spent $100 on a planner. I think that makes me sound absolutely insane and awesome at the same time. It's also really nice leather and it smells good, so I guess it is worth the money [laughs].

The planner really allows me to see the big picture, instead of getting focused on all of the little things. I have so many goals written down that I know what I am going to be doing, what I'm going to be making, and where I'm going to be living when I am 23. I have all this stuff written out. I figure out the outcome that I'm looking for and then I just work backwards to see what I need to do along the way. I think a big problem is that people don't always know what outcome that they want. If you don't know what you're looking for, then how the heck are you going to find it?

Q: What is the single most important reason for your success?
A: It's the combination of taking action, working my butt off, and then expecting it to work. You combine those things, and I think that you can't go wrong.

Q: What would you tell an up-and-coming entrepreneur?
A: Provide tons and tons of value for all of your prospects and customers. Completely over-deliver every time. Don't get bogged down with negative thoughts and thinking that it might not work. Just have an unwavering knowledge that it is going to work. The biggest thing, above all, is to take tons of action. Always be moving; never let inertia stop. Then, you really can't go wrong.

Alex's Favorite TV Show:
How I Met Your Mother

If you're looking to sell information products online, you're going to have a lot of challenges facing your potential success. No one knows who you are; no one trusts you; no one knows that your products are any good. If you're just starting, you probably don't have people to sell to either. The best thing that you can do is to launch your product. Don't just put it out there: actually do a real product launch where you get several different venture partners who tell their existing prospects and customers how awesome you are. There's your credibility. Have them send out emails and things like that, so you start to build a prospect list. Together, that solves a lot of the challenges that you have.

ALEX MAROKO

169

Q: If you had to battle a giant, what weapon would you use?

A: I would look at what weapons people had used in the past to be successful – anything from a sword to mind power. Maybe the best weapon is a dictionary to hit the giant over the head with. If that's what works, then I'll go for the dictionary.

That's exactly how I run my business. I see what works in other markets and then I model it, mess it around, and make it fit my own personality until it fits my market. Then, I throw it out there knowing that it's a proven method in these other markets. But I don't just copy it. You can't take something from one market, transfer it to another market, and just expect it to work. But you can see what works for other people and then adapt it to your own business.

Q: What do you want to be when you grow up?

A: I want to be cool. That would be the first thing I want [laughs]. Besides that, I really just want to lead a life on my terms. I don't ever want to be at a point where I can't do what I want to do when I want to do it. Having that type of freedom really speaks to me.

So I just want to continue to run and build my online

| *Alex's Favorite Movie:* |
| **Iron Man** |

business. I definitely want to have several different online revenue streams that for the most part automate themselves. I'll have a certain level of income guaranteed coming in every day and I could sleep and it would still come in. That way, when I am 24 or 25, most of the work is cut down to 30-90 minutes a day. Then I could use the rest of my time to focus on other hobbies, people, riding my jet ski – whatever.

On a bigger scale, I want to create this empire of really darn good sports training products that athletes all over the world will have access to and that will help them become better at their sport.

Q: What key events transformed you from a sports trainer to six-figure internet entrepreneur?

A: There are three things that come to my mind immediately. The first one was when I was 13 years old and I decided that I was going to be a college basketball player. I had just been cut from my eighth grade basketball team. I was an awful basketball player. So, looking back on it truthfully, that goal was completely ridiculous. But I'm glad I set it and I'm glad I believed in it because eventually it did come true. I spent the next years of my life basically learning, studying, and applying all of these different training techniques to improve myself as an athlete. Without that goal, I would have never collected all of the training expertise that I now have and use on a daily basis.

When I went to play college basketball in Florida, there was a trainer about two blocks from my college who was starting to build an online business as a football trainer. I found him online. I literally walked down to his gym, introduced myself to him, and now we're really good friends. He and another trainer pushed me to start my online business. They kept telling me, "Dude, you've got to do this. You're going to kill it." That was the second event.

It's really unbelievable: looking back on this, I'm realizing that this stuff is connected. It's kind of blowing my mind right now. But, the third event was when the other trainer who I met in Florida told me that Yanik Silver was giving away a scholarship to his Underground Online Seminar 5. He was 26, so he couldn't apply, but he said, "You're going to be perfect for this." At that time, I didn't even know who Yanik Silver was. So, I was very green in the internet marketing community. But, I applied and two weeks later I made it as a scholarship winner.

I went to the event and it was really, really life-changing – all

ALEX MAROKO

of the stuff I learned, all of the people I met. That was late February 2009 and two weeks later we launched our first product. We made $20,000 in a week. Since then, life has just been this awesome roller coaster that never seems to stop moving.

Q: How do you diffuse skepticism when selling your products online?

A: People are always, always, always going to have questions and objections about buying things. So, as they are reading your sales letter or watching your sales video you want to be already answering that objection – right at the point where they're saying, "What about this? What about that?" That's just basic marketing, to overcome their objections. You don't want to miss any of those.

Especially with online marketing, the biggest issue is trust. You build up your email list and then you merchant that list and you build trust with each and every single one of them. Once they see that the information you're giving works and they believe in what you say, it becomes really easy, because the distrust is gone. They feel like you're just an online friend of theirs and that what you're going to say will help them.

> *Alex's Favorite Band:*
> *Trey Songz*

At that point, you don't have to market any more. You don't have to be the snake oil salesmen who hard-sells them. You just have to recommend what you think that they should do. Once you build that trust, obviously you don't want to sacrifice it just to make more money by promoting bad products or putting out crap. You can't do that.

Q: How have the ladies reacted to your success?

A: They've reacted. But, the big thing isn't your success online or how much money you're making. I just think that women

NICK SCHEIDIES AND NICK TART

are attracted to ambition. It's not the money or the cars. It's the fact that you're driven and you have your own life. It's not like I walk around with a t-shirt that says, "I make a lot of money on the internet doing nothing." Though, I should test that out and find out the conversion rate [laughs].

Q: Anything else you would like to add?
A: Thank you for the interview. I've had a lot of fun with this and I appreciate it.

Website: GameSpeedInsider.com
Twitter: @alexmaroko

"I shouldn't have watched this video. Now I feel like going out and balling instead of sitting here on this computer and working. Great interview. Very inspiring. Setting goals is great and I like how he acted on his goal."

~ Ralph,
Comment on JuniorBiz

ALEX MAROKO

"The greatest reward in becoming a millionaire is not the amount of money that you earn. It is the kind of person that you have to become to become a millionaire in the first place."

- Jim Rohn

22

Miss Entrepreneur and Friends
Juliette Brindak, Miss O and Friends
Old Greenwich, Connecticut

BACKGROUND

Growing up in Connecticut, Juliette Brindak used to start bake sales, lemonade stands, and garage sales. But when she was ten years old, her entrepreneurial horizons expanded during a routine family vacation. Juliette created a series of drawings of girls, one of whom was named Miss O. Everyone liked the characters so much that she kept drawing them – and soon enough, her family joined in to help bring the characters to life.

In 2005, Juliette launched MissOandFriends.com, a by-girls-for-girls site where tweens can go to safely interact, get advice in a supportive community, and play flash games that range from fashion contests to mini golf. The Miss O characters offer positive role models for growing girls and they've been featured in a series of books that have sold over 120,000 copies collectively. In 2008, Procter & Gamble invested in Miss O and Friends and estimated the company's value at $15 million dollars.

Today, the Miss O and Friends team includes over 30 people – including 15 interns, a board of 12 people, a webmaster, a lawyer, a school psychologist, and Juliette's mom and dad. At 21 years old, Juliette is the spokesperson and a writer for the website. She's also going into her senior year at Washington University in St. Louis, MO, studying anthropology.

INTERVIEW
Q: What would you be doing right now if we weren't talking?

A: Sleeping. I usually stay up pretty late, so I wake up pretty late.

Q: What drove you above and beyond, to entrepreneurship?

A: I just had the passion to do something for young girls. That's what drove me. I had an idea that I was really passionate about and, with the help of my family and everyone that supports Miss O and Friends, I was able to get it out there.

I have the most amazing support from my family, my friends, my partners, and everyone we meet. People know we're making a positive impact on young girls' lives. That really is a huge driver for us. It's such a good feeling.

Maxine Clark is the founder and CEO of Build-a-Bear. When Miss O and Friends was in the early development stages, we were really trying to get momentum going and [Maxine Clark] was a huge supporter. She set up connections with investors and other people who she thought would be helpful to our company. She kept us going, especially me. We would not be where we are without her.

> *Juliette's Favorite Movie:*
> **Legally Blonde**

Q: How do you balance your business with other priorities?

A: It can be overwhelming, because sometimes everything falls at the same time. I'll have Miss O work, school work, and then I'll also want to go out with my friends. In high school, it was hard to do Miss O while applying to colleges. I don't think that it negatively affected me, but it was probably the most stressful that Miss O has ever been for me.

I used to be a huge procrastinator. But I've realized that I can't do that if I want to get stuff done. I have learned how to be really efficient. I work better when I work under pressure. So, sometimes it helps when I know, "I have to get this done if I want to do well in my test and still go out with my friends on Friday night." It's just about being really efficient with my time.

Q: What challenges have you faced specifically because of your age? How has your age helped you to succeed?

A: My young age didn't create any challenges. It actually helps me. When I would present to Colgate, Procter & Gamble, Yahoo, or Target, they would be shocked that a 16-year-old could present a company to them. I think that they were really impressed. At first, I thought that people wouldn't take it seriously – but because we have accomplished so much, I think that people really respect me for it.

Q: How have people around you reacted to your success?

A: They're all really excited for me. I have gotten ridiculous reactions like, "Let's get married!" I'm like, "What are you trying to say right now?" People are really happy when something works out. So, I have great support from my friends. I was actually interviewed at school once and my friends got to be in the segment. They were like, "Oh my gosh! I'm going to be on TV!"

When I first got to college no one knew about it. For a while, my best friends and roommates had no idea what I was doing. I never wanted to talk about it, because sometimes it gives me too much attention. Then, the school newspaper wanted to do an article on me and I was really reluctant. When I did it, everyone started coming up to me. It was kind of intimidating. But now it's fine and I think that people respect me a little bit more for it.

Q: How did you plan and organize your business?

A: When it first started, it wasn't a business. The characters of the Miss O girls started off as my drawings. It was basically a hobby that my mom, my sisters, and I did. Then, for my sister's eighth birthday, my mom made Miss O characters for all of my sister's friends and they went crazy. They loved them.

JULIETTE BRINDAK

I was 13 at the time, my sister was eight, and that's the time when things start to get a little bit rough for girls. There are cliques at school, along with changes physically and emotionally. Girls can be mean. Boys come into the picture and school starts to get important. It's just really stressful. So, I thought, "We should really start doing something for these girls." That's what drove me to start Miss O and then, once I did, I had the best support ever. My dad, who has been in business his whole life, got involved and he really, really helped to get the company going.

Q: What is the single most important reason for your success?

A: We're authentic and girls see that. They see that we're a genuine company – not adults telling girls what they should be doing. Miss O and Friends is by girls, for girls. It's other girls giving girls advice. Our community is always giving us feedback and we're always trying to cater to their needs, like what they want on the site or any kind of product that they want. That's the key to our success: we're giving girls exactly what they want.

Q: What would you tell an up-and-coming entrepreneur?

A: Find a team of people who believe in your idea just as much as you do. This can be hard because you usually believe in it more than anyone else. But if you can find people who think that what you're doing is great, they're going to do everything in their power to make it a success.

When people invest in our company or when we form partnerships, it's hard because we're all so attached. But sometimes we have to make that sacrifice to improve our company. When we give up some ownership, we're only giving it up to people who are really going to follow through and do everything they can do to help these girls succeed. It's a trade-off.

I think that it's easy to get too caught up in everything and be too emotional about your own company. You need to detach yourself a little bit. People are going to tell you that they don't like it and that you need to be doing something different. That can be really hard to hear. A lot of young entrepreneurs hear constructive criticism and they get completely discouraged – or they get angry and just write it off. You need to learn how to take criticism, think about it, and then maybe work it into your business.

Juliette's Favorite TV Show:
Glee

Q: If you had to battle a giant, what weapon would you use?

A: Battle a giant? When I think about the stereotypical view of a giant, they're not usually that smart. So, I would probably try to confuse it, trick it with words, or just lead it in the wrong direction. Like with Miss O and Friends, when I do presentations, I have to be very careful with what I say. It's not that I am trying to trick people or lead them the wrong direction. But my word choice is very important.

I've really learned how to be confident in my speaking. I was never really that shy, but I would get uncomfortable when I had to speak in front of people. But I knew the information so well about Miss O that I became confident. Miss O has really helped me when it comes to talking to people, understanding body language, and engaging people in what I'm saying.

Q: What do you want to be when you grow up?

A: I am trying out a bunch of different things. At first, I thought that I wanted to continue on to business school. But I feel like I've learned enough to start this company and be successful on my own, so I kind of cut that plan out. Then I wanted to be a writer, because I do a lot of writing with Miss O and I love to write. I was an English major.

Now, I've switched my major to anthropology and pub-

JULIETTE BRINDAK

179

lic health. I definitely want to do something in the medical arena. I'm going down to [Washington,] DC this summer to intern at Georgetown hospital, just to check out that field. Medical school is definitely an option. Public health is definitely an option. With Miss O, I've done something that really helps people and I want to continue that with whatever path I take.

> **Juliette's Favorite Website:**
> **Shopbop.com**

Q: Did you ever expect Miss O and Friends to get this big?

A: We had absolutely no idea. It started out as a hobby for my mom, my sister, and me to play around with. We knew that girls loved what we were doing, but I had no idea that my drawings from a family vacation could turn out to be a company, let alone a successful one.

When we first started, we just wanted to do licensing. We wanted to sell Miss O stationary, clothing, games, and that type of thing. But, when we actually launched our website in April 2005, it grew our company into something completely different. That was the most critical step. It was before Facebook, MySpace, and Twitter had taken over. We saw a gap in the market for girls and we filled it. Our website *is* Miss O and Friends now. Without it, we would be nowhere.

Q: How did get your brand into over 20,000 classrooms?

A: The very first article that was ever released about Miss O and Friends was in *Time for Kids*. It's a little in-class magazine for kids in middle school. On the back, there was a picture of me and a little blurb about Miss O and Friends. After that article hit, our traffic shot up. It was right when our website launched, so it was the perfect timing for people to find out about us. That's really how we got into the school system.

With our books, we got into the Scholastic Book Fair because they believed in what we were doing. They liked our books. If you look at the statistics for our site, about 50% of our traffic comes from word of mouth. It's mostly girls typing in www.MissOandFriends.com, as opposed to going to Google and searching "girls websites" or "dress-up games." Girls telling girls (word of mouth) — that's how we've expanded.

We've also had some press. I've done some TV interviews, magazines, and newspapers. That's another way that people are finding out about us. We've never had to have an agent or a publicist to get us into magazines or newspapers. People come to us, saying, "I've heard about Miss O. We would love to do a story on you."

> *Juliette's Favorite Band:*
> *Earth, Wind & Fire*

Q: Procter & Gamble has already invested in your company and you're seeking other major investors. How do you make decisions when it comes to investment?

A: Right now, we want to continue to build our website, launch our Miss O Virtual World, and actually – for the first time ever – spend money to get the word out. But, in order to do those things, we need a substantial amount of money. You have to pay people to code and to make the games. So, when we really want to expand our site, that's when we'll really start to look for investment money.

We've had a lot of different investors. One man on our board had connections with Procter & Gamble and he set up the initial meeting. They loved what we were doing and decided to invest. My dad is so dedicated to this company now and he is always networking with people. He's always trying to find someone who wants to invest. Right now, we are in discussions with a few potential investors. We need to find people who we can trust. They need to be passionate about our company and what we are doing: helping tween girls build self esteem.

JULIETTE BRINDAK

Q: Anything else you would like to add?

A: Finding a good support team is really the key to being successful. You have to find people who really believe in what you're doing. Once you do that, you'll do great things.

Website: MissOandFriends.com
Twitter: @missoandfriends

"I think having a support system isn't talked about enough in business circles. You have to have people around you believing in not only what you're doing but who you are, as well. When you're putting in the long hours of hard work, it can get overwhelming. Having those small little reminders from those around you ("I'm proud of you," "stick with it," "you're making progress") can be really motivating."

**~ Chase B,
Comment on JuniorBiz**

MISS O AND FRIENDS

23

Inspired Designer for Hire
Jacob Cass, Just Creative Design
Brooklyn, New York

◆

BACKGROUND

As an Australian teen, Jacob Cass first began making money on-line as an eBay seller, but his true love was graphic design. Jacob nabbed his first freelance job at the age of 16. In November 2007, he started a website and blog dedicated to his business, Just Creative Design. He immediately began raking in clients, awards, and recognition. Not satisfied with one successful blog, Jacob launched LogoDesignerBlog.com and LogooftheDay.com to further preach his passion.

In January 2010, after earning a degree in graphic design, Jacob received a job offer from an unlikely source: his Twitter account. He packed his bags and moved from Sydney, Australia to Brooklyn, New York, where he currently works for Carrot Creative – a marketing agency that focuses on new media design and development. With what little free time he has, Jacob enjoys travelling and listening to music.

INTERVIEW

Q: What would you be doing right now if we weren't talking?

A: Right this second, I would be working on an identity design for a client. That's what I was doing before this. I keep busy.

Q: What drove you above and beyond, to entrepreneurship?

A: I just wanted to do more with my life – and I was going to need money in order to do what I wanted to do with my life. So at the start, what really drove me was the money.

That's when I started my first business, selling stuff on Ebay. I was earning money but I really wasn't enjoying it as much as my hobby, which was design. Once I figured out that I could make money with design, I went down that road, learned how to be a freelancer, and started my own business.

> **Jacob's Favorite Website:**
> **Twitter**

I've always had supportive parents. They've put a roof over my head for a good part of my 22 years and they've inspired me to keep doing what I like doing. They have their own businesses, so I was pretty lucky in that regard as I could get motivation from them. Back in school, I wasn't the most focused student, though I soon became more focused. Once I knew what I actually liked doing, I realized that it wasn't a chore. I found my passion in design and it just seemed natural to go in that direction.

Q: How do you balance your business with other priorities?

A: It was always a challenge to figure out my priorities, between work, university, friends, and family. Friends and family always came first, I think. A lot of the time, I just wanted to have fun. During school, I was doing freelance work and blogging and that was taking up a lot of my time. My schoolwork suffered, but I think that I was learning more by working for clients outside of school. It was real world experience, so I kind of focused my efforts on that.

Q: What challenges have you faced specifically because of your age? How has your age helped you to succeed?

A: I once had a client who didn't find out my age until after they had hired me. They mentioned that they may not have hired me if they had known my age. In saying that, I've also had clients who have hired me because of my age. When I asked them why, it was because they wanted a "fresh, younger approach" to business. I guess your age can work for or against you.

Online, you don't really have to show your age. Some people like to conceal it. Personally, I'm pretty transparent with my business. I don't think there is any point in disguising my age. It's a matter of preference.

I use my age as a selling point, to show how motivated and passionate I am. The thing is, you have to have the work to back it up. You have to show your achievements and prove that you're better than other people who may have ten or more years of experience. It's not about how many years of experience you have; it's about the quality of your years of experience.

Q: How have people around you reacted to your success?
A: Success is quite subjective. I am successful in a way, but you never stop and say, "I'm successful." For my family, it became more of a reality when I got a job halfway across the world.

Two days ago, I got my first email from someone who wanted an autograph. I had no idea what to say. It's a bit nuts, isn't it? That was probably the weirdest reaction that I've had up to now.

Q: How did you plan and organize your business?
A: This is probably not the best question to ask me, because I never planned anything. I was just learning things and then implementing them. I started my blog when I had no idea what blogging was. I thought that blogging was writing up what you had eaten for breakfast. It was probably about six months until I really got a grip on everything online: WordPress, Google, SEO (Search Engine Optimization), and all of the social network sites.

There was no real planning when it came to how I was going to position myself. Clients just found me through my website, thanks to my high search engine rankings and use of

JACOB CASS

social media. That's how I built my business. It was just a website. I focused my business on identity design simply because that's what I liked to do.

Q: What is the single most important reason for your success?

A: My blog, definitely. I started in November of 2007, so it has been about two years and four months. The blog started out with no readers but it has slowly built up quite a following. I have learned so much from people who have come in and shared their experiences and advice. I learned more in six months of blogging than I did in three years at university.

Q: What would you tell an up-and-coming entrepreneur?

A: Do the research. I didn't. Before you put your feet in the water, know where you want to go and how to get there. Research what you need to do and how you need to do it. That's probably what I should have done in the first place.

There are so many blogs online right now that are just chewing up old articles and presenting them in a new way. You're not going to last a long time if you keep doing that. If you want to stand out and be a long-term thing, then be original. In blogging and design, create original content to really stand out.

Q: If you had to battle a giant, what weapon would you use?

A: I would pick up the nearest thing next to me, which would most likely be a keyboard. [In terms of my business,] my clients aren't giants. Small to medium-sized businesses are my clients, so I don't need to battle the giants. The giants go for bigger fish. So they're not really my competition.

Q: What do you want to be when you grow up?

A: If you asked me six years ago, I probably would have told you I wanted to be a sportsman. But now, I'm pretty happy where I'm at. I love design and I think I will be doing this for quite a long time. I don't have any set plans; I just take it as

JUST CREATIVE DESIGN

it comes. I never thought that I would be in New York a year ago.

Working at Carrot is a full-time job, so I'm pretty focused on that. I am going to slowly slow down my freelance work, because I realize that I'm up until midnight every night and then going to work at nine o'clock the next day. I'm still learning about how much I can take on and I now know that I have taken on too much. I'm still loving it. But it's my goal to get this work (if you can call it that) done, so I can enjoy the upcoming summer even more.

> **Jacob's Favorite TV Show:**
> **Family Guy**

Q: What challenges are unique to being a freelance artist?

A: As a designer and a freelancer you wear many hats. You're an accountant, a promoter, a marketer, a blogger, a writer – all of these things. The challenge is combining all of your skills to make a successful business and to be one well-rounded business person.

Pricing is another challenge. I didn't do my research at the start and I was charging way too low. Looking back on it, I was working for nothing, really. Pricing has been a gradual process for me. It's all about changing with the environment. You only have so many hours in a day, so you can raise your prices to reflect your experience and the number of clients wanting your services. It's all about supply and demand.

Q: You've earned 12 awards and 32 press mentions. How has this recognition affected your business?

A: Some of them have come to me. Some of them have come from my own submission. Awards are a good way of showing clients that your work is up there with the best, but I don't work for awards. If a submission wins, great: another trophy for the mantelpiece (or Pool Room for you Australians out there).

JACOB CASS

In the press, my biggest surprise was when I made the front page of my local newspaper [*The Newcastle Herald*] for being the "Top Twitterer in Newcastle." That was actually a big surprise, because I thought I would be somewhere in the back of the newspaper. Then, I went to purchase the newspaper and there I was on the front page. I never thought I would make the front page of a newspaper. That was pretty cool.

> *Jacob's Favorite Movie:*
> **Avatar**

Q: Anything else you would like to add?
A: No, that's all. If you want to find out more you can go to my main website, JustCreativeDesign.com. You can connect with me there.

Website: JustCreativeDesign.com, LogooftheDay.com
Twitter: @justcreative

> *"Job offer through twitter account! Great interview."*
>
> **~ Lakhyajyoti,**
> **Comment on JuniorBiz**

JUST CREATIVE DESIGN

24

Made $2.5 Million, Lost Even More
Andrew Fashion, beModel
Denver, Colorado

BACKGROUND

As a sixth-grader, Andrew Fashion and a pal figured out a way to transform their mechanical pencils into miniature rocket launchers. Unlike most boys, they weren't content merely using their invention to annoy teachers and fellow students. Instead, they started a business called Flaming Gold and handed out pieces of paper to their friends, advertising their goods. It netted them a couple of dollars a day – until their school banned the pencils.

Fast forward to 2005: Andrew had dropped out of high school and was spending his time developing websites online. After months of just scraping by, Andrew hit it big with ad revenue from his website, MySpaceSupport.com. He was pulling in $100,000+ checks every month. But after a few years of living the high life, the money stream from the site dried up and Andrew went from being a millionaire to being in debt.

Today, Andrew is living in Denver, CO. He's working hard to launch beModel.com, a social networking website inspired by his passion for the photography industry. He's also writing an autobiography that will detail his rise, fall, and resurgence. It is tentatively titled *Young & Stupid*.

INTERVIEW

Q: What would you be doing right now if we weren't talking?

A: This second, I would still be cleaning and tidying up the

ANDREW FASHION

house. I've got a few roommates living in my house. They help out and I help out, but I always have to clean up after them.

Q: What drove you above and beyond, to entrepreneurship?

A: In the beginning, it was about having all the toys. I was really into skateboarding and technology, so I always wanted the newest computer, the newest iPod, etc. The best of the best. Now it comes down to the fact that I just really want to be successful, make a lot of money, and live life to the fullest. I also love to help people, so it's kind of 'all of the above'.

I don't want to settle for a nine-to-five job. So, I'm constantly driven by the desire to do my own thing. I would rather end up living back at my mom's house or at a friend's house than get another job. That's how stubborn I am.

Q: What challenges have you faced specifically because of your age? How has your age helped you to succeed?

A: My age has never gotten in the way. I've heard a lot of people say that it's hard for people to take them as seriously because they're younger. I've never had that problem because people see me being so persistent and professional that they say, "This kid is really serious." I don't ever mess around, so I've been able to talk to business owners and investors without them ever mentioning anything about my age.

It's not always the old people who are wise. It's the new age. It's the vision. Younger people can see what's going to happen and what needs to happen. So, I think a lot of older people actually like the fact that I'm young. Lately, they seem to believe everything I say.

Q: How have people around you reacted to your success?

A: When I was making a bunch of money, my close friends were just in shock. A lot of people started trying to get close to me and pitch their ideas to me. I found out who my real friends were. Five of my friends backstabbed me. One of them stole $5,000 from me. This guy was a good friend for a year or two and we hung out often. Then he told me that he would give me a deal at a shop, because he worked at BMW. He ended up taking five grand. I definitely learned a lot. I have a lot of haters, I guess. But I also have a lot of people who are really positive and who are rooting for me.

Q: How did you plan and organize your business?

A: Back in the day, MySpace Support was all with Adobe Dreamweaver, [the web development application]. There was no business model needed with that one. I just started working my butt off promoting it on MySpace and getting people to advertise it. Eventually, it grew to an astronomical size.

> **Andrew's Favorite TV show:**
> **Lost**

ANDREW FASHION

beModel, on the other hand, I put a lot of work into. It started with a pen, a piece of paper, and an idea. Then I typed up an executive summary, a bio, and used Microsoft Excel for all of my projections and expenses. I had an editor go over everything to make sure it all sounded professional and that my writing was up to par for the investors.

I've read a lot about business. I'm an avid fan of the *Rich Dad* series, by Robert Kiyosaki. I took what I could learn [from the books] and did the best with what I could whip up.

Q: What is the single most important reason for your success?

A: I want to be known for something great and I want to be able to help people. I also try to stay as positive as I can. There is a movie called *The Secret* that I leave on loop almost every day. It's about the law of attraction and being positive. So I'm always reminded that, "If you want it, you can have it." That comes into play with the way I do business.

Q: What would you tell an up-and-coming entrepreneur?

A: You've really got to want it. If you want to build a business, you can't just say, "I want to build a business." You have to figure out exactly what you want to do and then do it. Believe that it's already happening. If you slack on it, no one is going to believe it. Do it. You cannot stop.

A lot of young people don't do the research to see if their idea is in a niche that has potential for growth. That's what I see all of my friends do around me. They say, "I want to do this, I want do that." But they're not doing it. They just say it. People stop before they even start.

Q: If you had to battle a giant, what weapon would you use?

A: That's a tough one. I would like to have powers. I would like to be Goku [from *Dragon Ball Z*] in this situation. So, I would want to do [the energy blast attack] Kamehameha. If I had to use an actual weapon, I think it would be cool to use a knife, like a ninja.

Q: What do you want to be when you grow up?

A: A real-estate developer – not an internet guy. I love the internet and I will always work with it, but my ultimate goal is to build casinos, hotels, and nightclubs. I'll start in the Denver area, open a night club with a partner, and then eventually I will move to Las Vegas and California to build some hotels and casinos. I want to be a skyscraper guy.

Andrew's Favorite Food: Pho

Q: You made 2.5 million dollars. What happened to it?

A: I bought my first car, in cash. I bought my house and had $80,000 of renovations done to it. I ended up buying seven cars total, a few for my friends. One of my friends wrecked a car; I wrecked a car. I paid for that out of pocket.

A lot of my money just disappeared. I had a girlfriend. I lost a lot of money in Vegas. I got into poker. I bought a lot of toys, photography equipment, technology, tons of clothes, and trips to places like London, Florida, and Hawaii. I was young and stupid. The money was coming in so strongly, but it went out just as fast. All of a sudden, my site dropped off of Google and the money just stopped.

Andrew's Favorite Movie:
The Count of Monte Cristo

This time, instead of blowing money on toys and cars, I am going to invest it back into the company or another company. I will do the typical saving, like 401(k)'s and rainy day funds. But before I even start my retirement account again, I'm going to invest: real estate, stocks, commodities – whatever I can do.

Q: Why are you so sure that beModel.com will be successful?

A: I've done my homework on our number one competitor. They have been growing at a phenomenal rate. I think they have eight-and-a-half million page views a day. But they're not monetized properly.

I've been in the industry for three years. I've been watching the ads; I've been seeing their page views; I know how loyal their clients are. In their forums, I've seen people complaining and looking for new places to go. That's why I am so sure. I am here to be to them what Facebook was to MySpace. I want to revolutionize things.

Q: Anything else you would like to add?

A: Don't give up. Carpe diem: seize the day, seize the opportunity. You've got to say that every single day. Make sure you never miss a moment and just go for it. Do it. Never give up. As simple as that sounds, that's really it. Make it happen now, not tomorrow. Tomorrow is a loser's excuse.

Website: beModel.com, YoungandStupidBook.com
Twitter: @andrewfashion

ANDREW FASHION

*"If you're not living on the edge,
you're taking up too much space."*

- Anonymous

25

YouTube's Mystery Guitar Man
Joe Penna, Mystery Guitar Man
Los Angeles, California

BACKGROUND

Joe Penna grew up on a little-trafficked street in São Paulo, Brazil. When his mother needed help getting more customers to come to her yard sale, Joe used the family computer to design signs that he then posted around town. It was his first taste of business. When Joe was 12, his family moved to the United States. Joe attended the University of Massachusetts to become a cardiothoracic surgeon, but he eventually dropped out to follow his passion for video.

After bouncing around working on local commercials and music videos in Boston, Joe decided to pack his bags for Los Angeles to start making YouTube videos full-time. His channel, called *Mystery Guitar Man*, features a new video every Tuesday and Thursday, usually combining Joe's love for music with unconventional video editing and black sunglasses.

Since getting started in June 2006, Mystery Guitar Man has amassed almost one million subscribers and over 76 million total views – making it the 13th most subscribed channel on YouTube. He has since launched a second channel, called *jp*. His videos, like 'Guitar: Impossible' and 'Root Beer Mozart', have won various awards and have been featured on television programs around the world. He recently directed his first nationally televised commercial, for McDonald's and Coke. Joe just turned 23 years old.

JOE PENNA

INTERVIEW

Q: What would you be doing right now if we weren't talking?

A: I would probably be checking my video. I just put up a video so I would be checking comments and stuff like that.

Q: What drove you above and beyond, to entrepreneurship?

A: I was in Boston, studying biology, then bioinformatics, and then biomedicine. I kind of jumped around in the sciences, but it just wasn't for me. I had been doing the kind of videos that everyone does in college – just for fun. I knew that I wanted to do something technical, but I didn't know exactly what I wanted. So I figured, why not try to do video full-time?

> *Joe's Favorite Band:*
> *AC/DC*

I started working on commercials, music videos, and stuff like that in Boston. It was low-level work, like being a production assistant. I was hoping that in 30 years I would work up to become a director or something. At the time, nobody was making money off of YouTube, but I kept doing YouTube just for fun. I guess it worked out.

For my YouTube videos, I take inspiration from everywhere in life. I see things around and I'm like, "Tape! What can I do with tape? Why not try making a bunch of Mini-Joes, tape them up on wall, and do a video of that?" So, I am always thinking of new ideas. Michel Gondry is a big inspiration for me too. He's a guy who directs really creative movies and music videos. He was the one who did *The Science of Sleep* and *Eternal Sunshine of the Spotless Mind*. Great movies.

Q: How do you balance your business with other priorities?

A: I'm glad that it's paying my bills, so that I can focus on it. Mystery Guitar Man is my full-time job. It's around 80 hours of work a week. On Mondays and Wednesdays, I make the videos. Then on Tuesdays and Thursdays, I upload them. That way, I have Fridays and the weekends off to be able to

MYSTERY GUITAR MAN

think of new ideas and to go out with friends. I try to keep a balance.

Up to this last week, I had been doing it all myself – which was a bit crazy. I finally got a guy who helps me to edit and shoot. He brings in the footage and does a rough cut for me while I'm working on the music, the concepts, and stuff like that. I now also have someone who answers a lot of my business emails.

If I had a full-time job, I would still be doing YouTube. If I had a kooky idea, I would still make a video about it. Where else can you do a video with phone books, with paper cut-outs of yourself, or with crazy amounts of Pop Tarts? YouTube is the only place where that's okay.

Q: What challenges have you faced specifically because of your age? How has your age helped you to succeed?

A: It's tough for people to take you seriously when you're young. I faced some problems when I was in Boston trying to get work in commercials and music videos. They would just look at me – especially before I grew the beard – and say, "How old are you, kid? Twelve?" But I just ignored those comments and kept going on with what I loved to do. Young and inexperienced go together in a lot of people's minds, but I think that's an unfair prejudice. People can be experienced and talented at a young age.

College just wasn't working out for me, because I had picked the wrong thing. But when I first quit, the only people who said that it was a good idea were my parents. I was like, "I want to do this crazy, creative thing and eventually I want to do YouTube full-time." My parents were like, "Give it a try. If it doesn't work out in a year, reconsider your options. But you're going to regret it for the rest of your life if you don't give it a try." At the time, I was making $900 a month off of YouTube with $850 in rent. So sometimes it was like, "Do

JOE PENNA

197

I pay Chase credit card this month? Or do I pay for Ramen noodles?"

Of course, us young people have a lot of stamina. We can make videos until six in the morning, like I have done sometimes. Also, a lot of my audience is younger. 40% of them are 13-17 year-olds and then 20% of them are 18-24 year-olds. Being young helps me to connect with them and understand what's going on in their minds.

Q: How have people around you reacted to your success?

A: My parents are super-proud of me. My dad knows more about my YouTube account than I do. Once he called me and said, "Joe, there is a bad comment on one of your videos. Go delete it right now." I was like, "Dad, it's three in the morning! I can delete it tomorrow." He calls me like, "Hey, your 13th [most subscribed] now! I've done the math: it's this many days until your 12th!" I'm like, "Thanks dad." My mom sends out everything that I do – like books, CNN, interviews – to family members. So, they're super-supportive of what I do.

At first, a lot of industry people were like, "You're crazy. You're going to end up on the street if you keep doing that sissy YouTube stuff." But since I moved to LA, a lot of my friends are doing the same thing that I do. People who were my friends back in high school and middle school are coming up to me, like, "I watch every one of your videos. It's so awesome!"

Joe's Favorite TV Show:
House

It's funny because, when people come up to me on the street – even if I've never met them before – they're like, "Oh hey, what's up man? How's it going?" People feel like they know me. If you watch someone who vlogs a lot, you get to feel like you know them. I've gone to YouTube gatherings where I've met somebody for the first time and been like, "I'm confused. Have I ever met you in person? Or have I only seen your videos?"

Q: How did you plan and organize your business?

A: I didn't have many friends back in the day. I just had a lot of time. It was a boring summer, once upon a time, when I was around 18 or 19. So I just watched video tutorials. I was curious about how Windows Movie Maker worked. After I got Windows Movie Maker down, I moved on to Sony Vegas and eventually Final Cut Pro, which is what I use today. I started using different software, like After Effects and Apple Shake, and I learned how to light and how to operate cameras. It was mostly through watching other videos or movies and wondering how they did it. Then I would watch the 'behind the scenes'.

Q: What is the single most important reason for your success?

A: I think there are a lot of factors that play into me doing well on YouTube. One of them is that I do music. So, if you're from the United States, Brazil, or the middle of Kazakhstan, you can watch my videos and enjoy them all the same. There's a little globe on my channel. The green parts are where people watch my videos. At first, I thought that it wasn't working because the whole map was green. Eventually, I figured out that people from all around the world are watching my videos. It's a blessing for me that I never expected.

Another thing is that – because it is what I enjoy doing – I put a lot of effort into making my videos. Every video of mine is different. I'm not like a newscast where you know what you're going to get every time. I try to keep it different, new, and lively. With a lot of other people, you can tell that it's not what they love to do. Maybe it's just a paycheck for them. I also put out content every Tuesday and Thursday so that people will come back to my channel, wondering what I have up next.

When I first got to America, I did my best to try to assimilate

JOE PENNA

199

and be as American as I could be – which was wrong for me. When you're young and impressionable, you try to fit in with everybody. But I finally embraced who I was and said, "I'm Brazilian and I love Brazilian things." Having a different perspective on different cultures really opens your eyes to being more global, more cultural – and that's what YouTube is.

Every video that I forget to say something in Portuguese, I get a couple hundred of comments, like, "Where's

> **Joe's Favorite Website:**
> **YouTube**

your Portuguese?!" So, I make sure that I put closed captions in Portuguese at the bottom of my videos. I want to get different languages, like German, Spanish, and Italian – just so that more people can start understanding my videos. I'm going to start contacting people who can work for me with those closed captions. I'm going to tweet it out.

I love doing things that are community-based. I do a lot of videos where I have people send in things, like pictures of them imitating me. Right now, I just got a puppy. So, in my last video I said, "What do you think the name of my puppy should be?" My video has been up for two hours and it has 7,000 comments already, with puppy suggestions. I'm going to read through as many as I can until I find one that I like.

Q: What would you tell an up-and-coming entrepreneur?

A: For anything in life, you've just got to keep at it until you're good. When you're first learning to play a violin, you're going to have the cats howling outside. When you first learn to play guitar, your fingers are going to hurt and it's going to sound really bad. Your parents are going to be the only ones who are going to put up with it. The same thing with video: a couple days ago, I just watched the first video that I ever did, back in 2001. I cringed at every cut, like, "Argh – why did I put a star wipe there? Not a good idea!" Everybody was bad at first. So keep at it.

I was doing YouTube for four years before anyone saw my videos, really. If you want to get more subscribers and fans, one thing that helps a lot is a schedule. Maybe you have a job or school, so you can't do a video every week. But try to do a video every two weeks or something like that.

Don't get into something just because you hear that people are making money from doing it. If you do YouTube and from the beginning you're thinking, "I'm going to be making six figures a month doing this! I'm going to be a super-famous person with a lot of money," then it's never going to work out for you. If you're not having fun, it's going to show in your videos. So, if you love playing music, play music. If you love singing, sing a song. If you love doing crazy stop-motion things, do that. Every single person I know who is successful at what they do is successful because they love doing it. It sounds so cliché, but you have to do what you love to do.

Q: If you had to battle a giant, what weapon would you use?
A: At the moment, I have a Sharpie, so that's what I would use. I would poke him in the eye with the Sharpie – not with the permanent part of it, of course.

If you're creative in the way that you approach the problems in your life, then you

Joe's Favorite Movie: Die Hard

can definitely overcome them. When I first moved to Los Angeles, I was making just barely enough money to get me through. But I looked around and said, "What can I do to make this situation better?" I saw that I had a camera, an internet connection, and a laptop. So, I started doing videos full-time. Once, I accidentally dropped a spoon on a cup of water, and it went "Doo doo doo." I was like, "Yeah – that's my next video, right there."

JOE PENNA

Q: What do you want to be when you grow up?

A: YouTube is working out for me for now. YouTube is nice because you can do whatever the heck you want. You can make a video using cups of water. But I know that I'm not going to be 55 years old and still saying, "Mystery Guitar Man here, guys! Thanks for watching my video!" That's not going to happen. So, you have to think of the next step and for me the next step is becoming a commercial/music video director.

> *Joe's Favorite Book:*
> **Salem Falls**
> *by Jodi Picoult*

McDonald's, Coke, Pop Tarts, and *Glee* have all approached me with offers for stuff. It's working out. McDonald's and Coke asked us, "How did you make 'T-Shirt War'?" And we were like, "Why don't we just do it for you?" So, now we have a commercial that's playing nationally in all of the United States, plus internationally in movie theaters and things.

Q: What is your favorite thing about YouTube and why?

A: I think the community aspect is awesome. Immediately after you post a video, you see a bunch of comments, like, "Oh, I love this, I love this, and you should have changed this." Having that immediate feedback is what I enjoy most.

Collaborations are always fun. You're working with your friends, so it's kind of like you're just playing around with your friends and coming up with kooky ideas. But, of course, there is also the business aspect of it. You put a link to their channel on the video and then maybe they put up a 'behind the scenes' or a second part of the video. It's cross-promotion: new people are finding you from their channel and vice versa. There's some rivalry on YouTube, but I don't think there should be. It's not like they're watching Shane [Dawson] and not watching me. They're watching Shane and they're watching me.

MYSTERY GUITAR MAN

A lot of people's videos are vlogging: it's just them talking to the camera. I wasn't doing that for a long time, so people saw me as some kind of machine that made videos. When I started doing the 30 second videos at the end, it let my personality show a little bit. I like to find creative ways to tell people about my life and I like making creative calls to action. I also started a second channel (*jp*) to put up the stuff that was like, "I'm just going to bust out my camera and put up whatever."

Q: What have you done to push your success past YouTube?
A: I'm finally incorporated now, so I can hire interns and give them college credit. I also sell t-shirts to help me out with the cost of lights and stuff. I'm starting to do stickers right now. I'm going to run a contest where I give away t-shirts if people buy my stickers. That will be fun. I also have different ways of marketing myself, like Twitter and Facebook.

If it wasn't for the ads on YouTube, people wouldn't be getting paid. I wouldn't be doing it twice a week. I would probably be a waiter or something. So, the ads are a necessary evil. A lot of people are putting a lot of work into what you see.

Q: Anything else you would like to add?
A: If you're not doing what you love to do, at least give it a chance. Give it some time, too. Don't think, "Oh this isn't working out and I've been trying it for a week! I'm going to try something else." I gave myself a year to try YouTube out – and it worked out for me. If you think that you are going to love something, give it a try. You're going to kick yourself in the butt for the rest of your life if you don't.

Website: YouTube.com/MysteryGuitarMan
Twitter: @mysteryguitarm

JOE PENNA

So What Does it Take?

To Make More Money than Your Parents

Did you forget to take notes? We've taken the liberty of summarizing and synthesizing the responses of all 25 young entrepreneurs into delicious, bite-sized morsels.

Bon appétit.

Q: What would you be doing right now if we weren't talking?

A: Whether they're networking, meeting with investors, developing their products, or researching their next move, these young entrepreneurs work hard. They're never bored. But they don't do it alone: many said they would be collaborating with a partner or team. Also, they love their sleep.

Q: What drove you above and beyond, to entrepreneurship?

A: Overwhelmingly, our interviewees credited their parents and family for encouraging them. Personal drive, a competitive spirit, and the desire to be different while making a difference ranked high. Many said that they felt compelled to follow their inner calling and realize their own unique vision.

Q: How do you balance your business with other priorities?

A: Family and friends were the number one priority for most of these young entrepreneurs, yet many also expressed regret that their businesses had interfered with those relationships. School caused its fair share of headaches (some took time off or opted for online classes), but most also asserted that it was crucial to their ultimate business success.

It's never easy, but the interviewees are able to cope with their busy schedules with a healthy dose of focus, organization, prioritization, and time management.

Q: What challenges have you faced specifically because of your age? How has your age helped you to succeed?
A: Legal hurdles (checking accounts, PayPal accounts, and ownership) were common complaints, along with receiving a general lack of respect and credibility. But the consensus was that these challenges could be overcome by anticipating them and exceeding expectations of professionalism.

Some said there were only benefits to their youth – like the ability to work long hours and to connect with other kids. Younger entrepreneurs tended to cite the advantages of press and free advice. The older ones touted the benefits of not having to worry about money and the insights from fresh ideas and perspectives, especially online.

Q: How have people around you reacted to your success?
A: The response, especially from close friends and family, was described as positive, supportive, but not usually full of over-the-top surprise or excitement. Those types of reactions are more common from complete strangers – who give everything from autograph requests to marriage proposals.

Unfortunately, success has attracted its fair share of jealousies, false friendships, and over-exposure. Therefore, many young entrepreneurs have been reluctant to broadcast their entrepreneurial acheivements within their social circles.

Q: How did you plan and organize your business?
A: Our interviewees started with little more than an instinct for business and an unwavering drive to succeed. Eventually, all of them have become experts in their fields through hard work, research, experimentation, and an open mind to learn from mistakes. Family and mentors provided guidance along the way.

The interviewees also stressed the importance of writing their goals and tasks down on something tangible, like a

NICK SCHEIDIES AND NICK TART

calendar, planner, whiteboard, or notebook.

Q: What is the single most important reason for your success?
A: Common responses include: determination, hard work, never giving up, ambition, execution, passion, and support from friends, family, and faith.

Q: What would you tell an up-and-coming entrepreneur?
A: It's essential to set clear goals and then act on them. Be humble, be honest, and have true passion for your business. More than anything, our interviewees encouraged budding entrepreneurs to be patient and never give up, even when they aren't met with success right out of the gate.

Q: If you had to battle a giant, what weapon would you use?
A: We asked this question hoping to gain some insight into how these young entrepreneurs battle bigger, more experienced companies and still manage to come out on top. Answers ranged from swords to guns, but most agreed that they wouldn't need a weapon: they'd rather use their cunning, creativity, or friendship to overcome adversity.

Q: What do you want to be when you grow up?
A: Whether 12 or 23, most of these young entrepreneurs know exactly what they want and how they are going to get it. Others relish not knowing what's around the next corner. All of them want to continue to pursue entrepreneurship, many want to be involved with real estate, and most have plans to leave a legacy and make a difference.

> **Editor's Note:** At press time, neither Nick Scheidies nor Nick Tart were making more money than their parents. Take their advice with a grain of salt.

*"A man is not old until
regrets take the place of dreams."*

- John Barrymore

BONUS INTERVIEW

Co-Founder of YoungEntrepreneur.com
Adam Toren, YoungEntrepreneur.com
Phoenix, Arizona / Vancouver, BC Canada

BACKGROUND

Adam Toren has been an entrepreneur since he was seven years old. In high school, he and his brother, Matthew, used to import stereos and magic kits from Hong Kong to sell back home in Vancouver. They soon began buying struggling businesses, like pool halls and printing companies, and then rejuvenating them.

They're still helping businesses today through BizWarriors.com, but they've also started helping young people follow in their entrepreneurial footsteps. In 1999, Adam and Matthew launched YoungEntrepreneur.com, which has become the largest website in the world dedicated to empowering and educating aspiring entrepreneurs. They've also written a book on the subject, entitled, *Kidpreneurs - Young Entrepreneurs with BIG Ideas*.

Today, Adam makes his home in Phoenix, Arizona. He's 35 — and we're including him here to provide a glimpse into the life, insight, and experience of an entrepreneur who has seen it all, but who's still young at heart.

INTERVIEW

Q: What would you be doing right now if we weren't talking?

A: Well, it's over 100 degrees here in Phoenix today, so I'd probably grab my iPhone and head for the backyard for a refreshing swim.

While out there I'd start preparing for my upcoming week to

ensure that my time is maximized. I try to only work three days per week. Scheduled meetings and conference calls usually fall on Tuesdays, Wednesdays, or Thursdays. I find those are the most productive days to get a hold of people, because many people are busy playing catch-up on Mondays and preparing for the weekend on Fridays.

Q: What drove you above and beyond, to entrepreneurship?

A: My brother and I discovered entrepreneurship at early ages, before either of us were nine years old. We realized quite quickly that an entrepreneur is a visionary, a risk-taker, and a builder of businesses.

We grew up learning the entrepreneurial lifestyle from our grandfather, Joe, who had been an entrepreneur all his life. He actually set us up on our first entrepreneurial venture selling these little stunt airplanes called Dipper-Do's at a local folk festival. He taught us the proper way to use the stunt plane to really wow the audience and we sold out of them before the folk festival was over. What a great feeling for a couple of kids seven and eight years old! So it began: the entrepreneurial bug had bitten us.

> **Adam's Favorite Food: Sushi**

We then went from mini-venture to mini-venture throughout our schooling years. From importing stereo equipment and magic kits from Hong Kong, we learned a lot and made some money along the way. Then, as soon as we graduated from high school, we took the money we had earned and bought a struggling billiard hall in an up-and-coming part of our town. This is where we learned the saying that you hear so often from entrepreneurs: "We poured our blood, sweat, and tears into that business." We built the billiard hall into quite the happening spot, with a stage for live jazz, a liquor license, and a small café within the location. We ended up getting a great offer to sell in our 12th month of being in business.

We took the offer, took a vacation, and then we purchased another struggling business in a totally different industry: printing and graphics. We employed the same philosophies and principles to overhaul and successfully brand this small company. We sold it during our 11th month in business for a nice profit. We took our graphic team with us and started a publishing/media company, which has been one of our main focuses for the past seven years. We own niche-market, luxury-lifestyle publications with a combined readership of over 300,000 per issue.

Some things have definitely stayed the same since our first business venture: our dedication, work ethic, determination, and our passion to help others start, manage, and grow successful business ventures.

Q: How do you balance your business with other priorities?

A: During our entrepreneurial years in high school, we always tried to come up with ideas that our friends and peers would find interesting. Car stereos and "boom boxes" were the big thing during our senior years of high school, which is why we put together our first import company and designed a catalog of all the items that could be ordered (the internet has made this a lot easier these days). My brother and I have always been best friends and business partners. Over the years, we have identified each of our strengths, which is why we know who handles what within our companies.

Q: What challenges have you faced specifically because of your age? How has your age helped you to succeed?

A: Sure, there were definitely a few challenges with being viewed as a young entrepreneur. But nowadays I feel that the "young" aspect has a fresh image, based on all the internet successes that we have become familiar with.

Starting a business and sustaining it, especially in its early

ADAM TOREN

stages, is a definite challenge regardless of age. The young entrepreneur sometimes finds it particularly difficult to translate entrepreneurial ideas into a working reality. However, with the right tools, guidance, approach, mentorship, and support, young entrepreneurs have a solid chance of reaching success. I recall raising money being very difficult for my brother and me when we started. This forced us to get extremely creative with our own bootstrapped financing (i.e. loading up the credit cards). It was definitely a risk, but also something that we had to tackle and overcome.

Now, when we mentor some of the younger aspiring en-

Adam's Favorite TV show: Dexter

trepreneurs on BizWarriors.com, we always remind them that being an entrepreneur takes you on an emotional rollercoaster ride. There are a lot of ups and downs in a typical entrepreneur's day. Before taking the exciting steps toward entrepreneurship, it's definitely worth thinking through your ideas and considering whether you have the typical characteristics of an entrepreneur. My brother and I have narrowed these down to (1) a go-getter outlook, (2) creativity, (3) focus and passion, (4) drive and ambition, (5) open-minded to taking calculated risks, (6) commitment and dedication, (7) belief in yourself and the tendency to thrive on independence, (8) ability to multi-task, (9) honesty and integrity, and (10) refusal to let failures defeat you and ability to learn from mistakes.

This list is not at all scientific, nor is it intended to be a blueprint for success. There are no hard and fast rules. Many entrepreneurs start businesses based on their passions, experiences and skill sets. Getting to know our specific niche and product was our main mission when starting our entrepreneurial ventures. Understanding our customers' wants and needs was the key to our growth.

YOUNGENTREPRENEUR.COM

Q: How have people around you reacted to your success?

A: People around me have seen that we're successful by the way that we help others. The fact that we are able to donate to great charities, inspire fellow up-and-coming entrepreneurs, share our knowledge, and motivate people is how we want others to view our success.

A lot of people seem to define success as some type of goal. I actually see success as the process we're going through during our entrepreneurial journey. Success is a combination of a handful of important things: happiness, health, wisdom, love of family and friends, a sense of accomplishment, influence, and fulfillment.

Q: How did you plan and organize your business?

A: This is exactly what my brother and I thought about two years ago when we wanted to find a book about entrepreneurship for my brother's daughter, who was eight years old. We couldn't find such a book, so we decided to fill the void with one of our own. The book, *Kidpreneurs - Young Entrepreneurs with BIG Ideas*, was published last fall.

The philosophy behind the book is simple: the future of our children begins with us. Most people say, "It's never too late." My brother and I say, "It's never too early." The benefits of an early introduction to the basic principles and the infinite rewards of entrepreneurship are massive. In *Kidpreneurs*, we feel we have managed to break down otherwise difficult concepts into fun-to-read bites that any bright-minded child can easily enjoy, understand, and implement in their own business venture.

All children share the inalienable right to become financially independent, whether rich or poor, city or suburb. Sharpening a child's entrepreneurial skills will equip him or her with the skills necessary to tackle a limitless future. There is no reason it cannot start at an earlier age. *Kidpreneurs* puts

ADAM TOREN

power into the hands of the future.

There are also other great organizations, like Junior Achievement. Both my brother and I volunteered our time and had the opportunity to go into high school marketing and entrepreneurship classes to assist the teachers with some real world stories. I think that due to the current economic climate and the demand for entrepreneurs, you will start seeing several more tools, support networks, and resources for the aspiring young entrepreneur.

Q: What is the single most important reason for your success?
A: Businesses are most vulnerable to failure during the first few years of launching, with something like 25% of new businesses calling it quits within their first year and 50% failing within their first three years. With statistics like this, it's important to believe in, test, plan, and implement your idea.

The real difference between any young entrepreneur and the person who sits in a cubicle all day could be as simple as possessing the guts, drive, and focus to go for it – the ability to sacrifice some of your time and money to get what you want out of life. It boils down to following your dreams. Some of us young entrepreneurs have the gift to be able to dig within to pull out that drive and focus right out of the gate, but for others it takes more time – or possibly too much time!

The difference always seems to comes down to one word: *action*. When my brother or I have an idea for a business venture, we take the necessary steps to bring our idea to fruition and, in doing so, we always seem to surround ourselves with the right people. So there are three things that I bundle into our "Success Plan": taking action, following our dreams, and finding the right people to help take our ideas to the next level. Those things have helped us achieve success many times over.

Q: If you had to battle a giant, what weapon would you use?

A: I would say these magical words: "Go-Go-Gadget Super Samurai." Then I'd become a samurai and thank Inspector Gadget later! If you are getting your butt kicked, it's probably a perfect time to talk to an expert. Sometimes mentors and experts don't look like what we expect. Whether it's your neighbor who owns his own small business and is a martial arts expert or the guy who breaks bricks with his head and attends your Friday night networking group – I'm always surprised by what people know. Even if these people are in a totally different niche than you, they may share a story that you can relate to, so always listen. If you're one of those "closet entrepreneurs" you may not get out that often to attend in-person networking events; in this case, sites like LinkedIn and YoungEntrepreneur.com can help guide you to some credible experts.

If you're ready to attack another "giant," then learn about him or her and prepare for battle. The best way to approach a new market is with determination, drive, and focus. However, that determination is best when it stems from plenty of research and due diligence to the opportunities and the competition. Do your research, do a double-back flip jump, and land into the battle arena armed and dangerous!

Practice is not always the most entertaining part of being a samurai, but it does help. If Jack Black can do

> **Adam's Favorite Book:**
> **Business Stripped Bare**
> **by Richard Branson**

it as the Kung Fu Panda, then you can practice too. If your goal is to sell more products online via your sparkling new e-commerce site, then you most likely need to do some tests on your layout vs. various conversion rates. You may need to continually change up your content and practice being timely with these updates to ensure a fresh, content-rich site. It's best to practice using your entrepreneurial nunchucks in a

ADAM TOREN

safe and secure environment before you arrive on the battle-field.

Stick to your business ethics *always*. Samurais wore elabo-rate armor and never stabbed anybody in the back; ninjas wore no armor and loved stabbing people in the back. Samu-rais were renowned for their great bravery and code of hon-or. We've all heard the many stories of overcoming adver-sity to achieve great success and these stories are surely not new. Who would've thought that a high school dropout who worked for his father's local bicycle repair shop would cre-ate the car company we all know today as Honda? By 1948, Soichiro Honda had started producing his first complete mo-torcycles and was president of his company, Honda Motor Company.

Respect and discipline will win in the long run. In the movie *The Last Samurai*, when the ninjas attacked the samurai vil-lage, they got their butts kicked. Both ninjas and samurais are skilled fighters; however, the samurai is more disciplined, diversified, and tougher than the quick and agile ninja. Ap-preciating and respecting every one of your customers will help your company's positive image, brand, and word of mouth develop at samurai speed. Get ready to be a winner!

Q: What do you want to be when you grow up?

A: My brother and I have some exciting plans in the works. We are working on creating a fund for young entrepreneurs, which will allow us to invest smaller amounts of capital ($5,000-$25,000) to assist in launching solid business ideas, while also providing the mentorship and support that all of us entrepreneurs need during our journey.

We've done a lot and plan to do a lot more. I think that my 18-year-old self would be very impressed with what my brother and I have accomplished so far in this chapter of our entrepreneurial life. Stay tuned for much more, though!

YoungEntrepreneur.com

Q: How do you think that your life would be different if you had never gotten involved in entrepreneurship?

A: Normally I can close my eyes and imagine just about anything. But honestly, my life without entrepreneurship is something that I can't imagine. I enjoy the daily challenges, the problem solving, and – of course – the successes that come with the ups and downs.

Q: Anything else you would like to add?

A: Thanks for inviting me to participate in such a great interview and what looks to be a superb collection of interviews. I'm looking forward to reading the book and spreading the word!

Website: YoungEntrepreneur.com, Kidpreneurs.org
Twitter: @thebizguy

ADAM TOREN

How to Start a Business

If you've just read this book, you're probably feeling empowered to blaze your own trail. We don't want all of that inspiration to go to waste, so we've busted out a free, online guide to starting your own business.

Below, you'll find an outline to success and a link to the guide. Use it to launch your product, service, internet business, or something nobody else has thought of yet.

1. **Have an Idea**
   Small, big, or kooky.

2. **Know the Ropes**
   Check out your market and competition.

3. **Plan your Success**
   Discover how you'll make your money.

4. **Legal Mumbo Jumbo**
   Everything from licenses to LLCs.

5. **Market your Business**
   Hone in on your target market.

6. **Reach your Customers**
   Let people know that you exist.

7. **Lift Off**
   Transform your plans into actions.

8. **Get it Done**
   Master the day-to-day.

9. **Find your Fortune**
   How to collect and manage your money.

10. **Grow**
    Earn a spot in our next book.

Let's Get Started: **JuniorBiz.com/Start-a-Business**

How to Make a Website

Today, no business is complete without a website. We've created a free, online guide that shows you exactly how to make a site just like Alex Fraiser's, Syed Balkhi's, and Michael Dunlop's.

Through simple strategies and step-by-step videos, we'll show you how to build your website into a place where you can launch a product, share your ideas, or even start an online business from the ground up. The best part: you can start right now.

1. **Have an Idea**
   Small, big, or kooky.

2. **Purchase Domain and Hosting**
   Where, how, and with coupons.

3. **Get WordPress for Free**
   Set it up right.

4. **Grab a Design**
   Cool site – no coding necessary.

5. **Organize your Site**
   A checklist for settings and structure.

6. **Optimize your Site**
   With plugins and analytics.

7. **Think Strategy**
   Create the content that your visitors want.

8. **Strike it Big**
   With social media and search engines.

9. **Keep your Visitors**
   Capture their info and keep them coming back.

10. **Strike it Rich**
    The four fool-proof ways to make money online.

Let's Make it Happen: **JuniorBiz.com/Make-a-Website**

ABOUT 50 INTERVIEWS

Imagine a university where not only does each student get a textbook custom tailored to a curriculum they personally designed, but where each student literally becomes the author!

The mission of 50 Interviews, Inc. is to provide aspiring, passionate, driven people a framework to achieve their dreams of becoming that which they aspire to be. Learning what it takes to be the best in your field, directly from those who have already succeeded. The ideal author is someone who desires to be a recognized expert in their field. You will be part of a community of authors who share your passion and who have learned first-hand how the *50 Interviews* concept works. A form of extreme education, the process will transform you into that which you aspire to become.

50 Interviews is a publisher of books, CDs, videos, and software that serve to inform, educate, and inspire others on a wide range of topics. Timely insight, inspiration, collective wisdom, and best practices derived directly from those who have already succeeded. Authors surround themselves with those they admire, gain clarity of purpose, adopt critical beliefs, and build a network of peers to ensure success in that endeavor. Readers gain knowledge and perspective from those who have already achieved a result they desire.

If you are interested in learning more, I would love to hear from you! You can contact me via email at: brian@50interviews.com, by phone: 970-215-1078 (Colorado), or through our website:

www.50interviews.com

All my best,
Brian Schwartz
Authorpreneur and creator of *50 Interviews*

ABOUT NICK TART

As you read this, Nick Tart is responding to emails, setting up meetings, writing the next article for JuniorBiz.com, and otherwise doing everything within his power to preach the good word of entrepreneurship to the next generation.

Either that, or he's watching Taylor Swift's YouTube videos on repeat.

Nick was first bit by the entrepreneurial bug at the age of 12, when he offered to help a neighbor mow their lawn. Six years later, Nick's lawn care business was providing service to about half of his neighborhood.

But when he began studying management and marketing at the collegiate level, Nick realized just how much more his business could have accomplished if he had known a bit more about entrepreneurship. JuniorBiz, LLC was born out of Nick's desire to make sure that kids grow up with every entrepreneurial resource at the tip of their fingers.

Nick became a published author in 2009 with JuniorBiz's first product: the *JuniorBiz Lawn Mowing Guide*. In May 2010, at the age of 22, he graduated magna cum laude from Colorado State University, with a degree in Business.

His tentative post-grad plans include conquering the world.

ABOUT NICK SCHEIDIES

Nick Scheidies has wanted to be a published author since before he knew how to write. But a book about youth entrepreneurship was not what he had in mind.

That changed once Nick began transcribing and editing the interviews in this book. Nick could feel the power of entrepreneurship and, more importantly, he felt empowered himself.

In April 2010, at 21 years old, Nick was inspired to launch Next Level Ink – a freelance service dedicated to helping other writers and entrepreneurs turn their vision into reality.

Nick plans to continue building Next Level Ink while pursuing a master's degree in English this fall (2010) at Colorado State University. He will also continue to passionately promote youth entrepreneurship as JuniorBiz's Chief Creative Officer.

In his free time, Nick enjoys friends, family, and making music.

Nick and Nick would love to hear from you:
Nick@50Interviews.com

Or Just Check Out their Misadventures Online:
YoungEntrepreneurs.50Interviews.com

Website: JuniorBiz.com   **Website:** NextLevelInk.com
Twitter: @juniorbiz   **Twitter:** @nextlevelink